Analytical Grammar

Level 1
Grammar Basics
Instructor Handbook

Created by R. Robin Finley

ANALYTICAL GRAMMAR.

888-854-6284
analyticalgrammar.com
customerservice@demmelearning.com

Analytical Grammar: Level 1, Grammar Basics Instructor Handbook
© 1996 R. Robin Finley
© 2022 Demme Learning, Inc.
Published and distributed by Demme Learning

All rights reserved. No part of this book may be reproduced, stored in a retrieval system, or transmitted in any form by any means—electronic, mechanical, photocopying, recording, or otherwise—without prior written permission from Demme Learning.

analyticalgrammar.com

1-888-854-6284 or 1-717-283-1448 | demmelearning.com
Lancaster, Pennsylvania USA

ISBN 978-1-60826-653-1
Revision Code 1122-B

Printed in the United States of America by The P.A. Hutchison Company
2 3 4 5 6 7 8 9 10

For information regarding CPSIA on this printed material call: 1-888-854-6284 and provide reference # 1122-07222024

Made in the USA
Columbia, SC
21 September 2024

Table of Contents

Get Started with Analytical Grammar
Welcome to Analytical Grammar vii
Getting Started viii
Potential Activities xi
Tips for Success xiii

Lesson-to-Lesson Instructions
Lesson 1: Nouns 1
Lesson 2: Articles & Adjectives 13
Lesson 3: Pronouns 25
Lesson 4: Prepositions 37
Lesson 5: Subject & Verb 51
Lesson 6: Adverbs 65
Lesson 7: Sentence Patterns 1 & 2 81
Lesson 8: Sentence Pattern 3 97
Lesson 9: Linking Verbs and Sentence Patterns 4 & 5 113
Lesson 10: Helping Verbs 131
Lesson 11: Conjunctions & Compounds 147

Lesson Diagrams **167**

Bibliography **201**

Level 1 | Grammar Basics

Level 1: Grammar Basics
Welcome to Analytical Grammar!

Children begin learning the grammar of their native language long before they can speak it fluently. Even a toddler knows that "Dad ate pizza" makes sense, while "Pizza ate dad" is silly! Unlike other subjects, we already know the grammar of our daily language—even if we don't know that we know it. The key, therefore, is two-fold:

- Apply labels to the different parts of speech and grammar. We know grammar; we just may not know the names of things or why they are organized in certain ways.

- Understand how to use different language and grammar in different situations. While formal situations call for more formal language, the grammar of our everyday, informal language is not incorrect. Correct grammar changes depending on the situation. Just as a person using informal slang might be judged in a formal setting, the opposite is true: using formal language in an environment where casual language is the norm would seem strange.

These two components combine to make us better writers and, therefore, better communicators. Consistent use of grammar and proper use of punctuation helps keep written information flowing easily to the reader. With a mature understanding of grammar, students are better able to share their increasingly complex thoughts and ideas in a clear, understandable way.

Getting Started

Some grammar "rules" are unbreakable. A sentence must always have a subject and a verb, for example. However, in many cases, rather than "rules," they should be looked at as "guidelines." Even professional grammarians (We do exist!) disagree on things like what a prepositional phrase is modifying in a sentence. Sometimes we even disagree with ourselves from day to day! This is okay. A sentence can be grammatically correct even if there is disagreement about how it is parsed or diagrammed. If your student has enough grammar knowledge to make an informed argument as to why they believe a certain answer is correct, it's a win—give them credit and move on.

The goal of each lesson is that students acquire enough familiarity with the topic that they can achieve 80% on the assessment. *Analytical Grammar* is intended to be an open-book curriculum, meaning that students are encouraged to use the lesson notes to complete all exercises and assessments, so this should not be a difficult goal if students are completing the exercises. Also, once introduced, concepts are repeated in each lesson, so perfect mastery is not required before moving on.

Grammar is a cumulative process. While new parts of speech will be addressed in subsequent lessons, students will continue to practice what they have already learned, and new skills will build upon that knowledge.

Analytical Grammar is just one component of a complete language arts program, which should include literature, writing, and vocabulary or spelling. By dividing the program into 5 levels, students are able to spend a short time of their school year focusing on grammar, then concentrate more fully on another component armed with the skills to improve their communication.

Components

Analytical Grammar is separated into five levels

Level 1: Grammar Basics: elementary introduction to the nine parts of speech
Level 2: Mechanics: elementary guidelines for punctuation and word usage
Level 3: Parts of Speech: complex information about parts of speech and their interactions
Level 4: Phrases and Clauses: advanced work with more complex components
Level 5: Punctuation and Usage: in-depth information about punctuation and word usage

For each level, you will need these components:

Student Worktext

- *Student Notes* provide instruction and examples for each topic
- *Exercises A, B, & C* give students plenty of practice in applying their new knowledge
- *Playing with Words* activities provide weekly instruction and practice with functional writing skills
- *Assessments* are always open book and provide an accurate measure of proficiency

Instructor's Handbook

- Page-by-page Student Worktext copy with solutions for all student work
- Instructor tips with additional explanation on possible points of confusion
- Item-by-item scoring guide for all assessments

11-Week Schedule

The study of grammar is just one part of a complete language arts program. Your student is expected to progress through the *Analytical Grammar* lessons at their own pace, then continue to practice grammar skills while studying another area of Language Arts.

Lessons

Week 1	Lesson 1
Week 2	Lesson 2
Week 3	Lesson 3
Week 4	Lesson 4
Week 5	Lesson 5
Week 6	Lesson 6
Week 7	Lesson 7
Week 8	Lesson 8
Week 9	Lesson 9
Week 10	Lesson 10
Week 11	Lesson 11

Instructor Notes

An *Analytical Grammar* Week

Most *Analytical Grammar* lessons are set up in the same manner: a page of notes, three exercises, a *Playing with Words* activity, and an assessment. The following is a suggested schedule for completing one lesson a week.

Monday

Read over the lesson notes with your student.

Have your student **complete Exercise A.**

- Work the first one or two sentences together, then have your student complete the rest.
- Remind them that they can use the lesson notes as needed throughout the week.
- Encourage them to ask for as much help as they need.

Tuesday

Review Exercise A.

- This should take no more than 20 minutes.
- Discuss only those mistakes that relate to the lesson you are working on.
  - For example, if you are working on Lesson 1, Nouns, just look at the words that are supposed to be marked. If your student has marked a verb as a noun, you can safely ignore it. These kinds of mistakes will correct themselves as students go through the program.

Have your student **complete Exercise B.**

Wednesday

Review Exercise B.

Have your student **complete Exercise C.**

Thursday

Review Exercise C.

Read over and discuss the *Playing with Words* activity.

Have your student **complete the *Playing with Words* activity.**

- Each of you should complete the "How Did I Do?" section on the following page. Compare your evaluation with your student's self-evaluation.

Friday

Have your student **complete the assessment.**

- Remind them that it is open book and they should use the lesson notes as much as necessary.

The following Monday

Correct the assessment together.

- You read out the answers as your student crosses out any incorrect answers.

- Then, using the scoring guide found in the Instructor's Handbook on the assessment key, total up the correct answers and record the score on the test.

Now, **introduce the next lesson** and start The Process all over again!

Potential Activities

Parsing

There are only nine parts of speech. Some parts will always have the same job in a sentence. Others can fill a variety of roles, depending on how they are used. Identifying the parts of speech helps to narrow down the roles they may play. You will never find an adjective acting as an object, for example. Adjectives are always modifiers. On the other hand, nouns can do many different jobs in a sentence. Identifying parts of speech is called *parsing*. This is the first step to identifying the *job* that a word is doing in a sentence, since it helps students to narrow down the possibilities.

```
 art  adj   adj    n     av    pp  art  n    pp  art   n
 The quick brown  fox  jumped (over the dog) (in  the road).
```

Short Answers and Fill-in-the-Blanks

Some exercises include short answer and fill-in-the-blank questions. These include activities like providing definitions, identifying a word's job in a sentence, and revising sentences to have proper punctuation.

Diagramming and "The Process"

Diagramming a sentence can strike fear into even the most experienced grammar student. That's why we break it down into an easy-to-follow series of questions that we call "The Process." In small increments, by answering yes/no questions about the sentence and its words, students learn to diagram increasingly complex sentences until they are confidently creating elaborate diagrams. Your student will be well prepared for the challenge. Some students enjoy the satisfaction of putting all of the parts of a sentence into their proper places.

We don't, however, diagram just for the sake of it. Diagramming visually demonstrates the structure of a sentence. It can clarify a relationship between two parts of speech like no amount of words can. While it is important to practice each new skill learned, once a student can demonstrate confidence with the part of speech, diagramming can be reduced, and you may find that your student doesn't need to complete every sentence in every exercise. It is simply a tool to support understanding of the parts that make up a sentence's structure.

Playing with Words

On the fourth day of each lesson, students will complete a *Playing with Words* activity. These activities are based on grammar, punctuation, or writing skills. They are usually directly related to the topic of the lesson and cover important concepts that will benefit students as they develop their writing skills. They provide a break from the lesson content, allowing students' brains an opportunity to store the grammar information they are learning in long-term memory. While these activities are intended to be fun and informative, they introduce and practice important skills and should not be skipped.

Instructor Notes

Assessment

On the last day of a lesson, students have an opportunity to show you and themselves what they have learned. They will be asked to complete exercises that are similar to the daily exercises. Points are assigned to each section; they are found in the Instructor's Handbook with the solutions. The points are intended to be a measuring stick for how confident the student feels about the material. Remember, your student can use their lesson notes to complete the assessment. They should not try to complete it from memory, without support. Before moving to the next lesson, the goal is for your student to receive at least 80% on the assessment. If your student scores less than 80%, we recommend you review that lesson's notes with them before introducing the next topic and provide heavier support as they begin the new lesson's exercises.

Notes on correcting assessments:

- When tallying assessment points, be sure to count the number correct. Don't count the number of errors and subtract it from the given number of total points. As your student acquires their grammar knowledge, they may mark a part of speech that shouldn't be marked in a particular lesson. Do not count these misplaced marks as incorrect. This problem will resolve itself in time as they progress through the program.

- For assessments with diagrams, you will notice that the diagrams in the solutions have check marks indicating what should be counted as a "point." Go through your student's diagram item by item and compare the checked items. If an item is in the correct place, make a checkmark. If it's in the wrong place, circle it so that your student can see where they made a mistake.

- For modifiers, if they are attached to the correct word and diagrammed correctly, count them as correct even if the word they are modifying is in the wrong place.

                art   adj   adj   n   av   pp   art   n   pp   art   n

Example: The quick brown fox jumped (over the dog) (in the road).

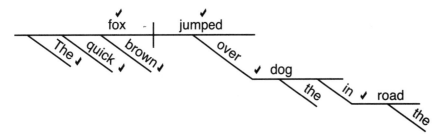

This diagram is worth seven points. Points are assigned for the subject (*fox*), verb (*jumped*), *fox*'s modifiers (*The, quick,* and *brown*), the prepositional phrase attached to *jumped* (*over the dog*), and the prepositional phrase attached to dog (*in the road*). Notice that although the prepositional phrases have three words, they each only have one check mark and therefore are worth one point as a unit.

Now, imagine your student diagrammed the sentence like this:

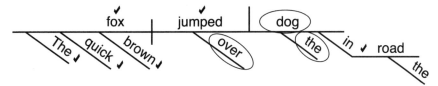

This diagram only loses one point. The prepositional phrase *over the dog* was only worth one point, so therefore it can only lose one point if it's incorrectly diagrammed. The prepositional phrase *in the road* still earns one point because it is correctly attached to *dog*.

Tips for success

This course can be adapted to meet your student's needs.

- If a lesson feels overwhelming and your student needs to slow down a little, have them do the odd sentences in an exercise one day and the evens the next.

- Consider only asking your student to diagram half of the sentences in an exercise. If they understand the concept and can identify the word, phrase, or clause that is the focus of the lesson, they do not necessarily need to diagram every sentence.

- On the other hand, encourage students to diagram at least one or two sentences from each lesson. Diagramming creates a visual image of how parts of speech interact. Allow them to choose which sentences they would like to diagram.

- Remind your student that they can look at the lesson notes for help as they are completing the exercises and even the assessment.

Lesson 1
Nouns

Instructor Notes

Students usually have an easy time recognizing nouns. Abstract nouns—things they can't touch or see—can be a little tricky for some. Don't be worried if that happens; just keep moving forward. Once learned, concepts are used in every subsequent lesson, so they will get plenty of practice and eventually, things will click. There are some cases where nouns are used as adjectives; for example, "birthday party." They will learn about adjectives in the next lesson, so let these kinds of mistakes go for now. If they mark pronouns as nouns, that's okay, too. This confusion will clear up after they learn about pronouns in Lesson 3.

Lesson 1: Nouns

The first part of speech that we're going to talk about is one of the most common: the **noun**. That's because we have to have a name for everything. If nothing had a name, how could we talk about anything? Have you ever tried to say something, but your brain can't think of the right words for it fast enough? That's when we end up using all sorts of crazy words like *thingamajig* or *whatchamacallit*. Imagine how confusing life would be if we didn't have names for all of the things we need to talk about!

> A **noun** is the name of a person, place, thing, or idea.

Think about the people you know. The words you use to talk about them are all nouns: *boy, girl, teacher, Mom, Dad, sister, brother, neighbor.*

Now walk over to the window and look outside. All of the things you can see are nouns: *house, school, street, tree, neighborhood, sidewalk.*

Now look around inside the place where you are. What do you see? Yes, these things are all nouns, too: *table, chair, desk, book, pencil, cat, dog, picture, kitchen, classroom.*

The nouns that we have listed are all things we can see and touch, but many nouns can't be seen or touched. They are **ideas**. This is a little harder, but can you think of any ideas that are nouns? Here are a few examples to get you started: *happiness, love, thought.*

All of the ***things*** in our lives are nouns. Even things we can't touch are nouns. Think about your feelings. You can't touch *love* or *anger* or *laughter,* but they sure are real things!

Sometimes we need to name the things we do. When you take the dog for a walk, you can touch the *dog*, but can you touch the *walk*? No, you can't, but the *walk* is still a thing. When your mom gives you a hug, can you touch the *hug*? It's still a real thing even though it can't be touched.

There are two kinds of nouns.

Most nouns are **common nouns.** A common noun is a noun that names a whole **type** of thing. For example, *girl* is a name for a whole type of human being, and *building* is the name for a whole category of structures.

There are two things to remember about common nouns:

1) Common nouns begin with a lowercase letter.

2) Common nouns are only made up of **one word**, such as *park, table,* and *cat.*

Proper nouns are the other kind of noun. Think of the names of some of the people you know. You don't just call them "boy" or "teacher." People's names are part of the group of nouns called **proper nouns**. A proper noun is a name that is given to a specific person or place or thing.

There are two things to remember about proper nouns:

1) Proper nouns begin with capital letters: *Simon, Julia, Fluffy, Mount Rushmore, the Nobel Prize.*

2) Proper nouns can have more than one word in them: *the Empire State Building, George Washington Carver, Longview Elementary School.* No matter how many words are in a proper noun, it only counts as one noun.

Nouns: Exercise A

Directions

Read the sentences below. Ask yourself, "What are the *things* in this sentence?" When you see a word that is a noun, write a letter *n* above it. The first one is done for you as an example.

The words marked with asterisks (*) are pronouns, but students may mark them as nouns. If they do, don't mark it as incorrect. In fact, if they mark them as nouns, that means that they are really thinking about the jobs that these words are doing in the sentence. Pronouns are introduced in Lesson 3, and this confusion will be resolved at that point.

                                 n   *n*   *n*   *n*

Example: The teacher read the class a really good story from a big book.

       n   *n*

1) My friend was having a party.

      n   *n*   *   *n*

2) The kids in our neighborhood all went to his house.

     n   *n*   *n*   *   *n*

3) His mom made a cake with candles because it was his birthday.

         n   *n*   *   *n*

4) After the children ate the cake, they played some games.

       n   *n*   *n*

5) In one game, a boy wore a blindfold.

       n   *n*   *n*   *n*

6) On the wall was a picture of a donkey with no tail.

   *   *n*   *n*   *   *n*

7) He had to pin a tail on the donkey while he was wearing the blindfold.

Short answer

8) Which kind of noun begins with a capital letter? _____

     a proper noun

1 EXERCISE B

Nouns: Exercise B

Directions
Read the sentences below. Ask yourself, "What are the *things* in this sentence?" When you see a word that is a noun, write a letter **n** above it, just like you did in the last exercise. Remember that some nouns are *ideas* that can't be touched or seen!

The words marked with asterisks (*) are pronouns, but students may mark them as nouns because they have not yet learned about pronouns. If they are marked as nouns, don't mark them as incorrect.

1) The _n_class went on a _n_trip to the _n_woods.

2) _*_They got the _n_idea from a _n_movie about _n_camping.

3) The _n_group was filled with _n_happiness at the _n_thought of _*_their _n_adventure.

4) The _n_children and _*_their _n_teachers loved the _n_beauty of the _n_forest.

5) The first _n_night, _*_everybody had a huge _n_appetite for _n_dinner.

6) One _n_boy ate three _n_hamburgers and got an upset _n_stomach.

7) After _n_dinner, the _n_group was in the _n_mood to hear _n_stories.

8) _n_Shouts of _n_laughter were heard until _*_it was _n_time for _n_bed.

9) The _n_children didn't have _n_homesickness because _*_they were having a good _n_time.

                        n   *n*   *n*
10) Great friendships grew from this journey into the wilderness.

Fill in the blank

11) A _____ consists of only one word.
         common noun

Nouns: Exercise C

Directions
Mark the nouns just as you did in the last two exercises. This time, be on the lookout for proper nouns. Write **n** over the common nouns and **pn** over the proper nouns. If a proper noun has more than one word, you will use "wings" to mark all of the words that make up the proper noun. Look at the example to see what nouns with "wings" look like:

Example: ——pn——   n   n   ——pn——
Mrs. Chen gave the class a homework assignment on Abraham Lincoln.

The words marked with asterisks (*) are pronouns, but students may mark them as nouns because they have not yet learned about pronouns. If they are marked as nouns, don't mark them as incorrect.

   pn   n   n   n
1) Alvaro, the boy who lives across the street, has a new dog.

      n   n   pn
2) The name of the dog is Ralph.

   pn   pn   n
3) Alvaro got Ralph as a birthday present.

     n   pn   ——pn——
4) His dad adopted Ralph at the Downtown Animal Shelter.

——pn——   n   ——pn——   pn n   n
5) Ms. Jensen at the animal shelter told Mr. Contreras to feed Ralph food for adult dogs.

 *   pn *   pn   n
6) I asked Alvaro if I could take Ralph for a walk.

   n *   ——pn——   n   n
7) On our walk, we saw Officer Brady, the police officer on the corner.

——pn——   pn   n   n
8) Officer Brady welcomed Ralph to the neighborhood and shook his paw.

    *   *pn*   *n*   *n*

9) I think Ralph is the best dog in the world!

Fill in the blank

10) A _____ noun begins with a capital letter and may be made up of more than one word.
  proper

1 PLAYING WITH WORDS

Playing with Words

The reason we learn about grammar is so that we can become better writers. In each lesson, we will take time to use what we have learned and practice our new skills. You will be asked to complete a few activities. Before you begin, read the next page, called "How Did I Do?" It will tell you how to get the most points possible on these activities.

1) Make up a sentence using the common noun *boy*. Write it below.

_____

_____

2) Make up a sentence using the proper noun *Mr. Ferguson*. Write it below.

_____

_____

3) Here is a list of nouns:

computer	*student*	*home*
homework	*printer*	*newspaper*
Janie	*table*	*pencil*
cat	*paper*	*Mr. Ferguson*

A) Talk to your instructor about the nouns. Are there any connections you can see?

B) On a separate piece of paper, write a paragraph of at least three sentences, using as many of these nouns as you can. Because this is a paragraph, make the sentences work together to tell a little story.

To see how you did on this exercise, look at "How Did I Do?" on the other side of this page.

Playing with Words
How Did I Do?

These "How Did I Do?" pages will give you a way to evaluate how well you completed the "Playing with Words" assignment. You and your instructor will both answer the questions and give yourself points depending on what you wrote. Then compare how many points you each think you earned.

Answer the following questions based on your student's work on the previous page. Then compare your answers with your student's.

1) If your sentence uses the noun *boy* and makes sense, give yourself two points.   _____

2) If your sentence uses the proper noun *Mr. Ferguson* and makes sense, give yourself two points.   _____

3)

If your paragraph has:	Give yourself
3 sentences or more	3 points
2 sentences	2 points
1 sentence	1 point

_____

If your paragraph has:	Give yourself
all 12 nouns	3 points
10 or 11 nouns	2 points
8 or 9 nouns	1 point
7 or fewer nouns	0 points

_____

Now, add up all the points for your **total points**:   ══════════

If you got 10 points, you did amazingly!

If you got 9 points, you did incredibly!

If you got 8 points, you did wonderfully!

If you got 7 points, you did a great job.

If you got 6 points, you made a good try.

1 ASSESSMENT

Nouns: Assessment

Directions
Write **n** over the common nouns and **pn** over the proper nouns. Remember to use wings to mark proper nouns with more than one word. You can look back at the lesson notes if you need help.

The points shown are the total possible points for each sentence. Remember to only count the number of correct answers. If a word is marked as a noun but it is not a noun, do not count it against your student. Only count whether the words shown as nouns or proper nouns in the solutions are marked correctly.

$\frac{\quad}{4}$ 1) We have a new [n]boy in our [n]class, and his [n]name is [pn]Jaden Winston.

$\frac{\quad}{3}$ 2) [pn]Jaden moved to our [n]town from [pn]Buffalo.

$\frac{\quad}{3}$ 3) His old [n]school was [pn]Emerson Elementary, and he was in the third [n]grade.

$\frac{\quad}{4}$ 4) The [n]kids in our [n]class asked him to play [n]kickball with them at [n]recess.

$\frac{\quad}{4}$ 5) [pn]Ms. Freeman, our [n]teacher, gave [pn]Jaden the [n]desk next to mine.

$\frac{\quad}{3}$ 6) I helped [pn]Jaden with his [n]vocabulary words, and he helped me with [n]multiplication.

$\frac{\quad}{4}$ 7) [pn]Sara is having a [n]party for [pn]Valentine's Day, and she invited [pn]Jaden.

$\frac{\quad}{4}$ 8) [pn]Brandon shared his [n]candy with [pn]Jaden at [n]lunch.

$\frac{\quad}{4}$ 9) [pn]Jaden said he felt like a [n]part of our [n]class on his very first [n]day!

                     ——pn——   n   n   n
 __ **10)** Ms. Freeman praised our kindness and thoughtfulness to a new student.
 4

$\overline{\overline{37}}$

Fill in the blank

Each correct answer is worth one point.

__ **11)** A _____ noun consists of only one word.
 1   *common*

__ **12)** A _____ noun begins with a capital letter.
 1   *proper*

__ **13)** A _____ noun may consist of more than one word.
 1   *proper*

__ **14)** A _____ noun begins with a lowercase letter.
 1   *common*

$\overline{\overline{4}}$

$\overline{\overline{\overline{}}}$ *Total Points* $\dfrac{33}{41} = 80\%$
  41

Lesson 2
Articles & Adjectives

Instructor Notes

This lesson will show you and your student how much grammatical knowledge is already stored in their brain. That's because, if a student finds the nouns first and then goes back to each noun and asks "Which __(noun)__?", the articles and adjectives will practically jump out at them!

One potential issue could occur when a noun has more than one modifier in front of it, such as "the strong, athletic girl." If the student asks "Which girl?", they might answer "athletic girl," mark that adjective, and think that they are done. If this happens, prompt them to look again by asking them "Which athletic girl?" until there are no more possible answers. Then they will spot *the* and *strong*.

Lesson 2: Articles & Adjectives

You're going to learn a new thing in this lesson that will make it even easier to find nouns!

In English, we use certain words—usually found in front of nouns—that help give more information about that noun. These words are called *articles* and *adjectives*. Even though they have two different names, they do the same job: *modifier*.

> **Modifier**
> A modifier is a word that modifies, or gives more information about, another word in the same sentence.

Articles

There are only three **articles** in English, and we use them all the time. They are *a, an,* and *the*. Articles are a special kind of adjective that always comes in front of a noun. If you see an article, you know that there is a noun coming up! You will never see an article all by itself in a sentence; it always goes with a noun.

- Use *a* before a noun that begins with a consonant sound *(a dog)*.

- Use *an* before a noun that begins with a vowel sound *(an apple)*.

- *The* can be used with any noun. If you want to talk about a specific dog or a specific apple, use *the (the dog, the apple)*.

Adjectives

An **adjective** modifies (describes) a noun. There are a lot of adjectives in English. They almost always come before a noun. They can give us all kinds of information about that noun. Some examples of adjectives are *red, blue, tall, short, wide, narrow, fun, serious, big,* and *small*. There are many, many more.

How to find articles and adjectives

When you are looking for articles and adjectives in a sentence, the best way to start is by finding as many nouns as you can! Then, go back to the first noun in the sentence and ask, "What (noun)?" or "Which (noun)?" and say the noun that you found. Any words that answer that question will be either articles or adjectives. It is easy to recognize the articles, because there are only three of them. Mark them with **art**. All other words that answer one of those questions are adjectives. Mark them with **adj**. Let's use the following sentence to practice finding and marking them:

The older kids in our school are reading a terrific book.

1) First, mark all of the nouns that you can find with **n**:

          n   *n*   *n*

The older kids in our school are reading a terrific book.

2) Next, go back to the first noun *(kids)* and ask, "Which kids?" The answer is *"the older* kids." *The* is an article and *older* is an adjective. Now ask the same question about each of the other nouns in the sentence. When you are finished marking **art** for articles and **adj** for adjectives, this is what the sentence will look like:

art adj   n   adj   n   art adj   n

The older kids in our school are reading a terrific book.

Proper adjectives

A **proper adjective** is an adjective that's made out of a proper noun. We know that a proper noun is the specific name that is given to a person, place, or thing. For example, *John* is a proper noun. What if we were talking about a book that belongs to John? We would say *John's book,* and *John's* would be an adjective, because it answers the question "Which book?"

Now here is something else to think about: do you remember that proper nouns can consist of more than one word? Well, so can proper adjectives! If we were talking about *John Jacob Jingleheimer Schmidt's book,* then all four of those words, *John Jacob Jingleheimer Schmidt's,* would be counted as one adjective. Mark it ***adj*** just like any adjective. But like with proper nouns, use wings to include all of the words that make up a proper adjective.

```
―――――――――adj――――――――   n
John Jacob Jingleheimer Schmidt's  book
```

Articles & Adjectives: Exercise A

Directions
Write **n** over all of the common nouns. Write **pn** over the proper nouns (use wings if you need them). Then write **art** over all of the articles and **adj** over all of the adjectives. Look at your lesson notes if you need help.

1) *adj* Every *n* child in *art* the *n* world has *adj* their *adj* favorite *n* story.

2) *adj* Most *n* stories have *art* a *adj* good *n* guy and *art* a *adj* bad *n* guy.

3) *art* The ——*pn* Big Bad Wolf—— is *art* the *adj* bad *n* guy in *adj* many *adj* fairy *n* tales.

4) *adj* Mean *adj* old *n* witches are *art* the *n* villains in *adj* many *adj* other *n* stories.

5) *art* The *adj* main *n* problem is to get away from *art* the ——*pn* Big Bad Wolf—— or *art* the *n* witch.

Short answer

6) In a complete sentence, write the definition of a noun.

    A noun is the name of a person, place, thing, or idea. (answers may vary slightly)

7) Which type of noun begins with a capital letter and may consist of more than one word?

    proper noun

EXERCISE B **2**

Articles & Adjectives: Exercise B

Directions

Write **n** over all of the common nouns. Write **pn** over the proper nouns (use wings if you need them). Then write **art** over all of the articles and **adj** over all of the adjectives. Look at your lesson notes if you need help.

The words marked with asterisks (*) are pronouns, but students may mark them as nouns because they have not yet learned about pronouns. If they are marked as nouns, don't mark them as incorrect.

1) I love "The Ugly Duckling," a story about an ugly baby bird which becomes a beautiful swan.
   * — pn — art n art adj adj n art adj n

2) The little duckling is found beside a pond by a mother duck.
   art adj n art n art adj n

3) She thinks he is an ugly little thing, but she takes him into her family.
   * * art adj adj n * * adj n

4) The other little ducklings laugh at him because of his appearance.
   art adj adj n * adj n

5) During the entire summer, he stays away from the other birds.
   art adj n * art adj n

6) The grown-up ugly duckling discovers that he is actually a beautiful swan.
   art adj adj n * art adj n

Short answer

7) In a complete sentence, write a definition of *adjective*.

   An adjective is a word that modifies a noun or pronoun. (answers will vary slightly)

8) Articles and adjectives do the same job. What is the job called?

   modifier

Articles & Adjectives: Exercise C

Directions

Write **n** over all of the common nouns. Write **pn** over the proper nouns (use wings if you need them). Then write **art** over all of the articles and **adj** over all of the adjectives. Look at your lesson notes if you need help.

The words marked with an asterisk (*) are pronouns. If your student marks them as nouns, do not count them as incorrect.

1) Many kids love the old story of a wooden puppet who wanted to be a real boy.
      adj n   art adj n   art adj   n   art adj n

2) An old clockmaker makes himself a wooden puppet because he has always wanted a little son.
    art adj   n   *   art adj   n   *
    art adj n

3) He wishes on the evening star that his little puppet would become a real boy.
    *   art adj   n   adj adj   n   art adj n

4) The beautiful Blue Fairy grants his wish, and Pinocchio begins to move.
    art   adj   ——pn——   adj n   pn

5) The fairy tells Pinocchio that, if he is a good, obedient child, she will turn him into a real little boy.
    art n   pn   * art adj   adj   n *   *
    art adj adj n

Short answer

6) List the three articles in English:

   _____

   a, an, and *the*

7) If you have a noun and an article, which will come first in the sentence?

   _____

   the article

Playing with Words

So far, we have learned about nouns, adjectives, and articles. Articles are easy because there are only three in English—no more, no less. Sometimes, though, a word can be used as either a noun or an adjective! That's why it's important to analyze, or ask questions about, what the word is doing in the sentence.

                       adj   adj   n   n

Example: My little brother plays *football*.

In this sentence, *football* is a noun.

       adj   adj   n   pn

His *football* games are on Saturdays.

In this sentence, *football* is an adjective because it answers the question "Which games?"

Now you try it! Remember to look at "How Did I Do?" on the next page before you start so that you can see how you can get the most points possible.

1) Make up a sentence using the **noun** *dog*. Write it below.

_____

_____

2) Now make up a sentence using the word *dog* as an **adjective**.
(**Hint**: Think about the kinds of things that a dog needs every day.)

_____

_____

2 Playing with Words

3) Think of a noun that can be used as an adjective, too.

My noun is _____.

Write a sentence using your word as a noun:

_____

_____

Write a sentence using your word as an adjective:

_____

_____

4) Here is a list of words. Some of them are nouns, some of them are adjectives, and some of them can be used as either nouns or adjectives. Write a short paragraph of at least three sentences, using as many of these words as you can. Remember that this is a paragraph, so the sentences need to be about the same idea.

teacher	*beautiful*	*class*	*forest*	*story*	*nice*
her	*Mrs. Jones*	*Bobby*	*trees*	*tall*	*kids*
their	*path*	*interesting*	*book*	*big*	*his*
old	*day*	*night*	*dream*	*funny*	*Christie*

Now look at "How Did I Do?" on the next page to see how well you did!

Playing with Words
How Did I Do?

After you and your instructor answer these questions about your writing, compare and see if your answers are similar.

Answer the following questions based on your student's work on the previous page. Then compare your answers with your student's.

1) If you used the noun *dog* in a sentence which makes sense, give yourself one point. _____

2) If you used *dog* as an adjective in a sentence that makes sense, give yourself one point. _____

3) If you wrote a sentence using your word as a noun, give yourself one point. _____

   If you wrote a sentence using your word as an adjective, give yourself one point. _____

4) If your paragraph has three or more sentences, give yourself one point. _____

   If your paragraph's three or more sentences are about the same idea, give yourself one point. _____

If your paragraph has:

Number of words:	Give yourself:
20–29	4 points
15–19	3 points
10–14	2 points
Fewer than 10	0 points

Add up all of the points for your **total points**: ══════════════

If you got 10 points, you did amazingly!

If you got 9 points, you did incredibly!

If you got 8 points, you did wonderfully!

If you got 7 points, you did a great job.

If you got 6 points, you made a good try.

2 ASSESSMENT

Articles & Adjectives: Assessment

Directions
Write **n** over the common nouns and **pn** over the proper nouns. Write **art** over the articles and **adj** over the adjectives. Remember to use wings to mark proper nouns or proper adjectives that have more than one word. You can look back at the lesson notes if you need help.

The points shown are the total possible points for each sentence. Remember to only count the number of correct answers. If your student marks a word that is not marked in the solutions, do not count it against them. Only count whether the words indicated in the solutions are marked correctly. Words marked with an asterisk (*) are pronouns. If your student marks them as nouns, do not count them as incorrect.

__   adj   adj   adj   n   adj   n   art   adj   n   *
12   **1)** One favorite children's story of all time is about a beautiful princess who runs

            art   adj   n
         away from a wicked queen.

__   art   adj   n   ——pn——   *   **   adj   n
8   **2)** The wicked queen hates Snow White because she is jealous of Snow's sweetness

            adj   n
         and great beauty.

**The word jealous *is a predicate adjective, which has not been learned at this point. If your student recognizes it as an adjective, great! However, if they don't, do not count it as incorrect.*

__   art   n   ——adj——   n   ——pn——   art   adj   n
8   **3)** The queen plots Snow White's death, but Snow White runs away into the great forest.

__   art   n   ——pn——   art   adj   adj   n
9   **4)** In the forest, Snow White finds a charming little cottage, which belongs to

            art   ——pn——
         the Seven Dwarfs!

__   ——pn——   art   ——pn——   adj   n   *   *
11   **5)** Snow White and the Seven Dwarfs become great friends, and they help her get away

            art   adj   n   adj   adj   n
         from the evil queen and find her true love.

==
48

Fill in the blank

___ **6)** A noun is the name of _____ .
  1   *a person, place, thing, or idea*

___ **7)** A _____ noun begins with a lowercase letter and can consist of only one word.
  1   *common*

___ **8)** An adjective is a word that _____ .
  1   *describes or modifies a noun or pronoun*

___ **9)** The articles in English are _____, _____, and _____.
  3   *a, an, the*

$\dfrac{}{6}$

$\dfrac{}{54}$ *Total Points* $\dfrac{43}{54} = 80\%$

Lesson 3
Pronouns

Instructor Notes

It's usually very easy for students to understand the concept of a pronoun. It's another thing for them to be able to recognize one when they see it! For that reason, it's a great idea to spend some time allowing students to familiarize themselves with them. They don't need to memorize them, but they need to be able to identify a pronoun in a sentence.

Take the time to recite the lists of pronouns out loud as they are introduced. Slow this lesson down and spend ten minutes a day playing a word game like "hangman" or another word guessing game using one of the lists. Have them put the words in a pronoun group in alphabetical order. Give them a quiz asking them to list five or ten pronouns, but require that they list different pronouns each day. Ask them to name five pronouns that start with a certain letter. Have them sort selected pronouns by type. It will be important in advanced grammar lessons (such as subordinate clauses) to be familiar with different types of pronouns, because they provide clues to what is happening in the sentence.

This is also an important point to emphasize: students need to follow a certain process in identifying the parts of speech. Students **must** find the nouns **first**, **then** the articles and adjectives, and **only at that time** should they look for pronouns among the words left over. This will keep them from misidentifying pronouns (other than possessive pronouns) as adjectives.

Lesson 3: Pronouns

Read the following sentence out loud:

> Jack said Jack and Maria are going fishing this weekend, and Jack is going to use the new pole that Jack just bought.

What do you think? It sounds pretty silly, doesn't it? You had to say *Jack* over and over again!

Let's use a new part of speech to make it less silly: **pronouns.**

> Jack said he and Maria are going fishing this weekend, and he is going to use the new pole that he just bought.

That's better! We substituted the word *he* for all of those extra *Jacks*. Why do you think we couldn't substitute *he* for the first *Jack* in the sentence? That's right; we need to say *Jack* first so that the reader will know who *he* is.

A **pronoun** takes the place of a noun. It can do all of the jobs that a noun can do. We also need to learn another word, although it isn't a part of speech: **antecedent**. Remember how we had to say *Jack* before we could say *he*, so that we would know who *he* is? The noun being replaced later on has to be stated first, **before** we can use the pronoun. *Jack*, the noun being replaced by the three uses of *he* in our second sentence, is the **antecedent** of the pronoun *he*. All three uses of *he* have the same antecedent.

There are five kinds of pronouns: personal pronouns, demonstrative pronouns, interrogative pronouns, relative pronouns, and indefinite pronouns. You don't have to memorize them, but you do need to become familiar with them. That way, you won't have to keep flipping back to these lists when you need to identify one.

Personal pronouns (most of these refer to people):

I	me	mine	myself
you		yours	yourself/yourselves
he	him	his*	himself
she	her*	hers	herself
it		its	itself
we	us	ours	ourselves
they	them	theirs	themselves

Demonstrative pronouns (these point to something):

| this | that | these | those |

Interrogative pronouns (these ask questions and don't have to have an antecedent):

| who, whose | whom | which | what |
| whoever | whomever | whichever | whatever |

Relative pronouns (these introduce clauses that modify nouns):

| who/whom | what | which | that |

Student Notes

Indefinite pronouns (use these when we're not sure who or what we're talking about):		
each*	anybody	many*
either*	anyone	more*
neither*	anything	much*
one*	everybody	most*
some*	everyone	both*
any*	everything	few*
other*	somebody	several*
another*	someone	all*
none	something	two*, three*, and all counting numbers
	nobody	
	no one	
	nothing	

You need to be able to recognize these words as pronouns when you see them. It's a good idea to take some time practicing them. Read them out loud. Try putting them in alphabetical order. Play a word game with your instructor. Again, there's no need to memorize them, but be sure you know a pronoun when you see one!

In the lists above, did you notice that some of the words have asterisks (*) next to them?
That's because those pronouns can sometimes be adjectives. When you are looking at a sentence and identifying the parts of speech, it's important to mark adjectives before you mark pronouns. That way, when you are marking pronouns, you will have already marked these sneaky words as adjectives because they answer the question "What (noun)?" or "Which (noun)?" If you see one of these words, and it's not acting like an adjective, then it's a pronoun, and you will mark it with *pro*.

Look at these examples:

                  pn   *adj*   *n*
Example: Jack loaned me *his* book

His is acting like an adjective, because it answers the question "Which book?"

                  pn   *art*   *n*   *pro*
Example: Jack said the book was *his*.

In this sentence, *his* is a pronoun. It takes the place of *book* and doesn't modify any other word.

Remember: If it acts like an adjective, mark it as an adjective. If it acts like a noun, it's a pronoun!

3 EXERCISE A

Pronouns: Exercise A

Directions

This exercise includes pronouns from the **personal pronouns** list.

Be sure to mark the words in this order!

- Write **n** over all of the common nouns and **pn** over the proper nouns (don't forget wings if you need them).
- Write **art** over the articles and **adj** over the adjectives (remember the wings for proper adjectives if you need them).
- Write **pro** over the pronouns.

In the space below each sentence, write the **pronoun** and its **antecedent**. Look at the example to see how, and remember that you can look at the lesson notes if you need help. (Be careful—one sentence has two pronouns and two antecedents! Can you find both?)

                      pn   *pro*   *n*   *adj* *adj*   *n*

Example: Janie said she was going to play soccer during this school year.

                  she = Janie

     art   *n*   ———*pn*———   *pro*   *art* *adj*   *n*

1) The students from Longfellow Elementary School knew they wanted a softball team.

    they = students

    art   *n*   *art*   *n*   *pro*   *art*   *n*   *n*

2) The players on the team were chosen, and they had a meeting to make plans.

    they = players

    pn   *pro*   *art* *n*   *art* *n*   *pro*   ———*pn*———

3) Hong said he thought the team needed a coach, so he asked Mr. Gardner.

    he, he = Hong   This sentence has two pronouns with the same antecedent.

   ———*pn*———   ———*pn*———   *pro*   *pro*   *art*   *n*

4) Mr. Gardner told Stephanie Ruiz that he thought she should be the pitcher.

    he = Mr. Gardner   she = Stephanie Ruiz

Exercise A

          art   n   pro   n   art adj   n   art   n

5) The pair of them had tryouts for the other positions on the team.

    them = pair

Short answer

6) Which type of noun begins with a capital letter and may consist of more than one word?

_____

a proper noun

7) Which type of noun begins with a lowercase letter and consists of only one word?

_____

a common noun

3 EXERCISE B

Pronouns: Exercise B

Directions
This exercise is about **interrogative pronouns**. Write **n** over the common nouns, **pn** over the proper nouns, **art** over the articles, **adj** over the adjectives, and **pro** over the pronouns. There may be personal pronouns in the sentences, too, so be on the lookout. Because interrogative pronouns often don't have antecedents, you don't need to worry about identifying those for this exercise. Look back at the lesson notes if you need help identifying any of the words.

      pn   pro   pro   art adj   n   n

1) Dad asked, "Who wants me to explain a few things about football?"

   pro   art adj   n   pn   pn   pro   art   n   art   n

2) "That is a good idea, Dad," said Joey. "What is the point of the game?"

    art   n   art   n   art adj   n   pro

3) "The purpose is to move the football to score the most points, and that

           n   pro

is done by gaining yardage," he said.

   n   art   n   art n pn   art   n   pro

4) "Yardage is the distance on the field," dad said, "and the team which gains

   pro   art adj   n

more gets closer to the end zone."

   pro   art   n   art adj   n   adj   n   pro

5) "Whoever moves the ball across the goal line gets six points," he explained.

Short answer

6) In a complete sentence, write the definition of an adjective.

_____

An adjective is a word that modifies a noun or pronoun.

Pronouns: Exercise C

Directions
This exercise focuses on **indefinite pronouns.** Write **n** over the common nouns, **pn** over the proper nouns, **art** over the articles, **adj** over the adjectives, and **pro** over all of the pronouns. There may be personal pronouns or interrogative pronouns in the sentences, too, so be on the lookout. Because indefinite pronouns usually don't have antecedents, you don't need to worry about identifying those for this exercise. Look back at the lesson notes if you need help identifying any of the words.

1) *pro* *n* *pro* *pro*
   Anybody can play sports, regardless of who they are.

2) *pro* *pro* *art* *n*
   All of us were born with the desire to move and work and play.

3) *adj* *n* *pro* *pro* *pro* *pro* *pro*
   Team sports and those that we do by ourselves are good for us.

4) *pro* *pro* *n* *pro* *art* *pro**
   All of us can find enjoyment in one or the other.

5) *adj* *n* *pro* *pro* *art* *adj* *n* *pro* *pro*
   Whichever sport they choose, anybody can have a healthier body with one of them.

Fill in the blank

6) The articles in English are _____ , _____ , and _____ .
   a, an, the

7) The article will always be located _____
   the noun.
   in front of

---

*Pronouns can be modified by articles and adjectives, too. If a pronoun "takes the place of a noun," then a pronoun can do anything a noun can do.

3 PLAYING WITH WORDS

Playing with Words

The points for each activity are given below.

1) Read these sentences carefully:

> Ms. Smith and Mr. Jones decided to take a drive in Mr. Jones's car. Ms. Smith asked Mr. Jones to put the top down on Mr. Jones's car, since it was a lovely day. Mr. Jones agreed and the top was lowered. As Ms. Smith and Mr. Jones drove merrily down the highway, Ms. Smith's hair was blowing all across Ms. Smith's face, and Ms. Smith did not have a hair tie for Ms. Smith's hair. Mr. Jones smiled, took off Mr. Jones's necktie, and said, "Here! Tie this around Ms. Smith's hair!"

These sentences sound kind of silly, don't they? Why? (*two points*)

_____

_____

On a separate piece of paper, rewrite the paragraph above and use pronouns so it doesn't sound so silly. (*two points*)

2) Now read this paragraph:

> John and Jason were just sitting on Jason's front porch on a very hot Saturday afternoon. John said, "John has an idea! John and Jason should go to the pond go to the pond for a swim!" Jason agreed that John had a great idea, and Jason went into Jason's house to get Jason's swimsuit and a towel. Next, John and Jason went to John's house to get John's stuff. John and Jason walked quickly through the woods to the point, and when John and Jason got there, John and Jason were in for a surprise. There at the pond, swimming happily, were John and Jason's dads! "Come on in!" John and Jason's dads yelled. "It feels great in here!"

This paragraph sounds pretty silly, too, doesn't it? Cross out some proper nouns and replace them with pronouns to make it sound better. Use as many pronouns as you can while making sure that the passage still makes sense. (*two points*)

When you corrected this paragraph, did you have a problem that you didn't have with the first paragraph? What is it? Explain the problem on the lines below. (*two points*)

_____

_____

3) Two words that sound alike but are spelled differently and mean different things are *it's* and *its*. Do you spot the difference between the two? *It's* has an apostrophe to show that letters are left out. It means either *it is* or *it has*. *Its* is possessive, meaning "something that belongs to *it*." Look at the following sentences that show the difference:

> **It's** - It's a beautiful day today. (*It is a beautiful day today.*)
> **Its** - The goldfish swam around in its bowl.
> (*The goldfish swam around in the bowl belonging to it.*)

Here are two more words that sound alike but are spelled differently and mean different things:

> **you're** (meaning *you are*)
> **your** (meaning *belonging to you*)

Can you write two sentences using these words correctly? (*one point per sentence; two points total*)

To see how you did on this exercise, look at "How Did I Do?" on the other side of this page.

3 PLAYING WITH WORDS

Playing with Words
How Did I Do?

After you and your instructor answer these questions about your writing, compare and see if your answers are similar.

Answer the following questions based on your student's work on the previous page. Then compare your answers with your student's.

1) The paragraph sounds silly because you don't need to keep saying *Ms. Smith* and *Mr. Jones* over and over. You can use pronouns instead. If your answer is correct, even if you use different words to say it, give yourself two points. _____

   If you rewrote the entire paragraph using pronouns where you could, give yourself two points. _____

2) The extra problem you have with this paragraph is that both people in this paragraph are boys. That means that you can't always just say *he*, *him*, or *his*, because it could mean either boy. If your answer is correct, give yourself two points. _____

   If you corrected the entire paragraph using pronouns where you could, give yourself two points. _____

3) If you wrote a sentence using *you're* correctly, give yourself one point. _____

   If you wrote a sentence using *your* correctly, give yourself one point. _____

   Add up all of the points for your **total points**: ══════════

If you got 10 points, you did amazingly!

If you got 9 points, you did incredibly!

If you got 8 points, you did wonderfully!

If you got 7 points, you did a great job.

If you got 6 points, you made a good try.

Pronouns: Assessment

Directions

Write **n** over the common nouns, **pn** over the proper nouns, **art** over the articles, **adj** over the adjectives, and **pro** over all of the pronouns. Remember to look at the notes if you need help.

$\frac{}{5}$ 1) If *pro* you think *pro* you can do something, *pro* you often *pro* can do *pro* it.

$\frac{}{7}$ 2) Once, a *art* boy *n* was told that *pro* he *pro* had been chosen for the *art* basketball *adj* team *n*.

$\frac{}{9}$ 3) Because he *pro* thought he *pro* must be a *art* good *adj* player *n*, he *pro* worked harder to develop

skills *n* that *pro* would help him *pro*.

$\frac{}{8}$ 4) He *pro* had no *adj* idea *n* that *pro* he *pro* was really only an *art* average *adj* player *n*.

$\frac{}{8}$ 5) Whatever *pro* you *pro* may think about it *pro*, the *art* boy *n* became a *art* better *adj* player *n*.

$\overline{\overline{37}}$

3 ASSESSMENT

Fill in the blank

___ 6) A noun is the name of a _____, _____, _____, or _____.
4
      person, place, thing, idea

___ 7) An adjective is a word that _____.
1
      modifies a noun or pronoun

___ 8) The kind of noun that begins with a lowercase letter and consists of only one word is
1
     the _____ noun.

      common

___ 9) The articles in English are _____, _____, and _____.
3
      a, an, the

═══
9

═══ *Total Points* $\dfrac{37}{46} = 80\%$
46

Lesson 4
Prepositions

Instructor Notes

Prepositions are usually a fairly easy part of speech for students to understand. Most prepositions will fit neatly into the sentence "The mouse goes _____ the box." The ones to be careful about are the ones that don't fit. Students will remember these through a memory trick. Spend some time on these prepositions, and consider giving a little quiz or playing a game to help your students remember them, either writing them down or saying them from memory.

Point out the prepositions that are more than one word. That list is on the second page of the student notes.

This is also your student's introduction to diagramming. It is a process that gradually steps up in difficulty, and its usefulness will become more apparent as you go on.

Finally, the concept of words having "jobs" is a focus starting with this lesson. In the exercises and the assessment, there are underlined words. Students are asked to identify which words are modifiers and which are objects of the preposition. This is introduced in Exercise B, so consider completing the first couple of sentences together for that exercise.

Diagramming solutions are found at the end of the book.

Lesson 4: Prepositions

Close your eyes and visualize each of these sentences as your instructor reads them out loud:
> I will see you before lunch.
> I will see you at lunch.
> I will see you after lunch.

How are these three sentences different from each other? Yes, in each sentence, the time when I will see you has changed. It is at a different **time**.

Now, visualize these sentences:
> The package under the tree is mine.
> The package in the tree is mine.
> The package near the tree is mine.

What changes in each of your mental pictures? That's right! The position of the package is different. It has moved to a different **place** in each sentence.

These are the words that changed in these sentences: *before, during, after, under, in, near*. These words are called **prepositions**. This is the new part of speech that we will learn about today.

> **Prepositions**
> A **preposition** is a word that shows the position or relationship of a noun to another noun. Sometimes it describes the position or direction in space (*near, to, above*) and sometimes the relationship in time (*before, until, since*). Sometimes it shows other kinds of relationships. (Did you notice that the word **preposition** has the word *position* in it? That's a helpful way to remember what prepositions do!)

How to find a preposition
First, make sure you find all of the nouns, articles, adjectives, and pronouns before you look for the prepositions. Then, look at the words that are left over and find the prepositions! How do you do that? Well, it's easier than you think!

Most prepositions will fit into the following sentence:
The mouse goes _____ the box.

Take each of the prepositions that we used in the sentences above: *under, in, near, before, during, after*. They all work in the blank except *during*, don't they? The Mouse-Box sentence will help you find almost all of the prepositions in sentences. But what about the ones that don't fit?

There are nine very common prepositions that don't fit into the Mouse-Box sentence, but don't worry. You may not remember them, **But Al Does!** Here's what we mean:

B = but	**A** = as	**D** = during
U = until	**L** = like	**O** = of
T = than		**E** = except
		S = since

All of these words are prepositions even though they don't fit into the Mouse-Box sentence.

When you are labeling words, prepositions are labelled with **pp**.

Prepositional phrases

A word may fit into the Mouse-Box sentence, or be one of the But Al Does words, but it's not a preposition unless it is in a **prepositional phrase**. To find a prepositional phrase, first find the word you think is a preposition. Then say the preposition and ask "what?" The noun or pronoun that answers the question is doing the job of **object of the preposition**. Here's what we mean:

I will see you **before** lunch.

I think that **before** is a preposition, so I ask, "before what?" The answer is "before **lunch**." Now I know for sure that **before** is a preposition because it has an object of the preposition: **lunch**.

The prepositional phrase includes the preposition, the object of the preposition, and any articles or adjectives that modify the noun. Here is the list of the prepositional phrases in the example sentences above:

> before lunch
> during lunch
> after lunch
> under the tree
> in the tree
> near the tree

Diagramming

Now you know enough parts of speech to begin **diagramming**, or drawing a picture of what jobs words are doing in a sentence and how they fit together. We'll start by diagramming prepositional phrases. A diagrammed prepositional phrase looks like this:

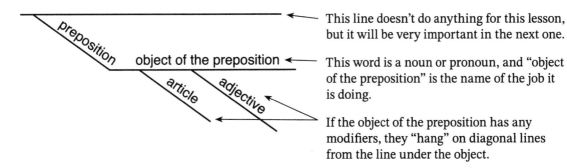

— This line doesn't do anything for this lesson, but it will be very important in the next one.

— This word is a noun or pronoun, and "object of the preposition" is the name of the job it is doing.

— If the object of the preposition has any modifiers, they "hang" on diagonal lines from the line under the object.

Just like words have jobs to do, **phrases** (groups of words working together) can have jobs, too. **Prepositional phrases** only have one job: they are always **modifiers**.

Note: A few prepositions include more than one word:

> because of
> in spite of
> according to
> instead of
> out of

If you find one of these prepositions, label it *pp* and use wings to include all of the words, like you do with proper nouns.

Prepositions: Exercise A

Directions

Be sure to mark the words in this order!

- Write **n** over all of the common nouns and **pn** over the proper nouns (don't forget wings if you need them!).

- Write **art** over the articles and **adj** over the adjectives (remember the wings for proper adjectives if you need them!).

- Write **pro** over the pronouns.

- Write **pp** over the prepositions, and put parentheses around the whole prepositional phrase.

On a separate sheet of paper, diagram each of the prepositional phrases. Remember that you can look back at the lesson notes if you need any help. The first sentence has been done for you, as an example.

                    pp   n   pro   pp art   n

Example: (On vacation), everybody (in the family) relaxes.

   art   n   pp   adj   n   pp art   n

1) A vacationer can think (about different things) (for a change).

   pro   pro   pp   n

2) They can relax and renew themselves (on vacation).

   n   pp   n   art n   pp   n

3) Time spent (on vacation) is never a waste (of time).

   pp adj   adj   n   adj   adj   n   pp   n

4) (On warm summer days), many bright solutions (to problems) have been dreamed **up**

   pp art adj   n   pp art   n

(during a little snooze) (in a hammock).

EXERCISE A **4**

Short answer

5) All of the underlined words in this exercise are doing the same job. After you have diagrammed all of the prepositional phrases, look back at the notes for this lesson. What is the name of the job that all of these words are doing?

_____

object of the preposition

6) In sentence 5, the word **up** is not a preposition, even though it fits in the Mouse-Box sentence. Why not?

_____

It doesn't have an object of the preposition, or, it is not part of a prepositional phrase.

Prepositions: Exercise B

Directions
Write **n** over the common nouns, **pn** over the proper nouns, **art** over the articles, **adj** over the adjectives, and **pro** over the pronouns. Write **pp** over the prepositions, and put parentheses around the whole prepositional phrase. On a separate sheet of paper, diagram each of the prepositional phrases. Remember that you can look back at the lesson notes if you need any help.

1) Our *adj* family *n* is going (*pp* on *art* a *n* trip) (*pp* during *adj* spring *n* vacation).

2) *pro* It is *art* a *n* trip (*pp* to *art* the *n* lake) (*pp* in *adj* our *adj* new *n* camper).

3) *adj* Family *n* vacations have been improved (*pp* since *art* the *n* invention) (*pp* of *art* the *n* camper).

4) *adj* Our *n* camper has *adj* four *n* beds (*pp* in *pro* it) and *art* a *adj* little *n* bathroom (*pp* at *art* the *n* back).

5) Now *adj* our *adj* camping *n* trips are fun (*pp* for *art* the *adj* whole *n* family), thanks (*pp* to *adj* our *n* camper)!

Fill in the blank

6) A prepositional phrase begins with a preposition and ends with a

_____.

(Write the part of speech it ends with, not the job that word does.)

noun or pronoun

Directions

Each of the sentences above include an underlined word. The words are doing one of two jobs. Choose your answer from the two jobs listed and write what job each underlined word is doing.

modifier   *object of the preposition*

Sentence #	Word	Job
1	trip	*object of the preposition*
2	new	*modifier*
3	invention	*object of the preposition*
4	little	*modifier*
5	camping	*modifier*

4 EXERCISE C

Prepositions: Exercise C

Directions
Write **n** over the common nouns, **pn** over the proper nouns, **art** over the articles, **adj** over the adjectives, and **pro** over the pronouns. Write **pp** over the prepositions, and put parentheses around the whole prepositional phrase. On a separate sheet of paper, diagram each of the prepositional phrases. Remember that you can look back at the lesson notes if you need any help.

      pp adj   adj   n   pro   n   n   pro art   adj   n

1) (On my seventh birthday), my mom and dad gave me a wonderful present.

    pro   art n pp ———— pn ————

2) It was a trip (to Boston, Massachusetts)!

  pp adj adj   n   pro   pp art adj   n   pp art ——— pn ———

3) (On our first day), we went (on a walking tour) (on the Freedom Trail).

 adj   adj   n   pp art ——— pn ———   art adj   adj   n   pp ——— pn ———

4) My favorite place (on the Freedom Trail) was the small wooden house (of Paul Revere).

  ——— pn ———   art   adj   n   pro   pp   art   n   pro

5) Paul Revere was the American hero who rode (through the night) so he could

       art   n pp art   n   pp art   adj   n

    warn the people (of the arrival) (of the British soldiers).

Fill in the blank

6) A pronoun is a word that _____.
    takes the place of a noun

7) Articles and adjectives both do the job called _____.
    modifier

Exercise C 4

Directions

Each of the sentences above include an underlined word. The words are doing one of two jobs. Choose your answer from the two jobs listed and write what job each underlined word is doing.

modifier   *object of the preposition*

Sentence #	Word	Job
1	seventh	*modifier*
2	Boston, Massachusetts	*object of the preposition*
3	walking	*modifier*
4	wooden	*modifier*
5	night	*object of the preposition*

Playing with Words

Directions

Here are three prepositional phrases, followed by a sentence with three blanks. Choose which prepositional phrase should go in each blank to make a complete sentence that makes sense.

of my desk   **on the corner**   **for a minute**

I leaned my elbow _____ _____
                    prepositional phrase 1   prepositional phrase 2

and rested my eyes _____ .
                    prepositional phrase 3

Now look at "How Did I Do?" on the other side of this page to see how you did and to see how to get the most points possible for the rest of this activity.

Below are a bunch of prepositional phrases. On a separate sheet of paper, write a paragraph or two using as many of these prepositional phrases as you can. Because it's a paragraph, remember that all of the sentences must work together.

If you change the place or the time that something is happening, start a new paragraph. Each paragraph should be at least three sentences long. If you think of other prepositional phrases that you would like to use, go ahead!

to the beach	*in the truck*	*of his tail*	*for her toys*
from her dad	*with lunch*	*on the back seat*	*in the sky*
of the ocean	*on the sand*	*in her bucket*	

Playing with Words
How Did I Do?

After you and your instructor answer these questions about your writing, compare and see if your answers are similar.

Answer the following questions based on your student's work on the previous page. Then compare your answers with your student's.

1) The sentence that makes the most sense is, "I leaned my elbow <u>on the corner</u> <u>of my desk</u> and rested my eyes <u>for a minute</u>." If you have the same sentence, give yourself three points. If you have any other sentence, give yourself one point.

2) Does your paragraph (or paragraphs) have at least three sentences? Give yourself one point.

3) Does your paragraph (or paragraphs) make sense? Give yourself one point.

4) How many prepositional phrases (either from the list or that you made up) did you use?

If you used:	Give yourself:
10 (or more)	5 points
8 or 9	4 points
6 or 7	3 points
4 or 5	2 points
2 or 3	1 points
0 or 1	0 points

Add up all of your points to get your **total points**:

If you got 10 points, you did amazingly!

If you got 9 points, you did incredibly!

If you got 8 points, you did wonderfully!

If you got 7 points, you did a great job.

If you got 6 points, you made a good try.

4 ASSESSMENT

Prepositions: Assessment

Directions

Write **n** over the common nouns, **pn** over the proper nouns, **art** over the articles, **adj** over the adjectives, and **pro** over the pronouns. Write **pp** over the prepositions, and put parentheses around the whole prepositional phrase. On a separate sheet of paper, diagram each of the prepositional phrases. Remember that you can look back at the lesson notes if you need any help.

Correctly identified words and prepositional phrases are worth one point each.

$\frac{}{18}$ 1) Ask most adults (about their favorite memories) (of their childhood), and they will
      adj   n   pp adj   adj   n   pp adj   n   pro

probably tell you (about a family vacation).
        pro pp art adj   n

$\frac{}{20}$ 2) Once, (on a rainy day) (during vacation), my brother won our family's money
    pp art adj n   pp   n   adj   n   adj adj   n

(in a game) (of Tripoli).
pp art n pp pn

$\frac{}{23}$ 3) Groans (of agony) (from Dad) and crows (of joy) (from my brother) came (with
      n   pp   n   pp   pn   n pp n   pp adj   n   pp

every hand) (of the cards).
adj   n   pp art n

$\frac{}{15}$ 4) (After the game), the family begged my brother (on bended knee) (for money).
    pp art   n   art   n   adj   n   pp adj   n   pp   n

$\frac{}{14}$ 5) The good part (of the whole thing) was that we were only playing (with
    art adj   n   pp art adj   n   pro pro   pp

imaginary money)!
  adj   n

$\overline{\overline{90}}$

ASSESSMENT **4**

Fill in the blank

___ **6)** Pronouns are words that _____ .

   1   *take the place of nouns*

___ **7)** Adjectives are words that _____ .

   1   *modify nouns or pronouns*

=
2

Directions

Each of the sentences above include an underlined word. The words are doing one of two jobs. Choose your answer from the two jobs listed and write what job each underlined word is doing.

modifier   *object of the preposition*

Each correct answer is worth one point.

Sentence #	Word	Job
1	their	*modifier*
2	vacation	*object of the preposition*
3	every	*modifier*
4	bended	*modifier*
5	thing	*object of the preposition*

=
5

4 ASSESSMENT

Diagrams
Enter score from diagramming solutions here.

$$\frac{}{18}$$

$$\frac{}{115} \text{ Total Points} \quad \frac{92}{115} = 80\%$$

Lesson 5
Subject & Verb

Instructor Notes

To find the subject of a sentence, it is important that students stick to The Process that they are learning: first, identify the nouns; second, articles and adjectives; third, pronouns; fourth, prepositions and prepositional phrases with parentheses; fifth, look for verbs among the words left over. Finding each of these parts of speech is easy if they are marked in this order.

Emphasize that the subject of a sentence will *never* be found inside a prepositional phrase. A prepositional phrase is a **modifier**. In other words, it can act like an adjective and describe a noun. If it modifies a noun, it will tell you "Which?" about that noun. "My neighbor across the street" is an example, because the prepositional phrase "across the street" answers the question "Which neighbor?"

Be sure that your student understands what a command is. Each exercise includes a command so that students can become comfortable with them.

Each exercise also includes underlined words. Students will need to identify the job each of these words is doing in the sentence. They will now be able to choose from **subject, verb, modifier,** or **object of the preposition.**

Diagramming solutions are found at the end of the book.

Lesson 5: Subject & Verb

In this lesson, we're really going to get into diagramming! We use diagramming as a tool to understand how the parts of a sentence fit together. Let's start with the two most important parts of a sentence: the **subject** and the **verb**. They are so important that you can't have a sentence without them!

The **subject** is a noun or pronoun. You've already learned all about those.

The **verb** is a new part of speech. For this lesson, we are going to focus on **action verbs**. Action verbs express physical or mental action.

Physical action is easy: when you *jump, search, carry, run,* or *sit,* you're doing something.

What about mental action? Well, when you *worry,* you're doing something. When you *think,* you're doing something. When you *believe,* you're doing something. That's what mental action means.

Verbs have to have a **subject**—it's the noun or pronoun that is **doing the action** of the verb.

How do you find the subject? Look at the following example:

The white horse in the lead raced across the finish line.

- First, mark all the nouns, pronouns, articles, adjectives, and prepositions in the sentence (in that order!). Put parentheses around the prepositional phrases.

  art   adj   n   pp art   n   pp   art   adj   n
  The white horse (in the lead) raced (across the finish line).

- Then look at the words left over for a word that shows physical or mental action. In the example above, the only word left over is *raced.* Mark it with a *v* for verb.

  art   adj   n   pp art   n   v   pp   art   adj   n
  The white horse (in the lead) raced (across the finish line).

- Sometimes a word can look like a verb but do a different job. To be a real verb, it has to have a subject. Look at the sentence again and ask yourself "Who or what *raced*?" The horse, right? So *horse is* the subject of *raced.*

- Now we know that *raced* is a real action verb with a subject. Go back and write an *a* (for *action*) in front of the *v* you have already written.

  art   adj   n   pp art   n   av   pp   art   adj   n
  The white horse (in the lead) raced (across the finish line).

Handy hint: The subject will **never** be inside a prepositional phrase! The nouns in prepositional phrases already have a job: object of the preposition. That's why it's so important to mark all of the prepositional phrases before you try to find the subject.

> Words may do different jobs in different sentences, but they can only do one job at a time.

Diagramming the subject and verb

You've already done a little diagramming of prepositional phrases, but you may not have noticed that we always included a horizontal line above the prepositional phrase. (Ask to see your instructor's book if you're not sure what we mean!) That horizontal line is called the **baseline**, and it holds the **subject** and **verb** (plus some other things we'll learn about later). It will be the first line you draw for your diagram. Here's the baseline for the example sentence above:

Diagramming articles and adjectives

Now we want to put the articles and adjectives that go with *horse* into our diagram. Here's what that looks like:

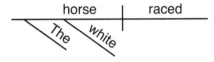

Articles and adjectives go on slanted (diagonal) lines under the noun or pronoun that the articles and adjectives modify, just like you learned when you were diagramming prepositional phrases. If there is more than one modifier under a noun or pronoun, put them in the same order in which they appear in the sentence. Make sure you capitalize the first word of the sentence, too!

Diagramming prepositional phrases

You already know how to do this! You just need to know that the diagram for the prepositional phrase goes under the noun or pronoun that it modifies. This is almost always the noun or pronoun **right in front** of the prepositional phrase. The prepositional phrase will answer the question "Which?" about that noun. In the sentence we have been diagramming, the prepositional phrase *in the lead* answers the question "Which horse?"

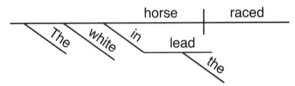

Diagramming commands

There is a kind of sentence called a **command**. It is used to tell someone what to do. In sentences like "Brush your teeth," or "Listen to me, please," it's easy to find the verbs. They are *brush* and *listen*. But if you ask "who or what *brush*?", where's the answer? It's there, but you can't see it! If your mom looks at you and says, "Brush your teeth," who is going to do the brushing? You are! The subject of a **command** is called an *understood "you."* You can't see it, but it's *understood* that the subject of the sentence is *you*. Look at the diagram. The *you* is in parentheses to show that it's *understood*; that is, it's not in the sentence, but it is still the subject that will do the action of the verb.

Remember, *Brush* is capitalized because it's the first word of the sentence!

5 EXERCISE A

Subject & Verb: Exercise A

Directions

Parse (mark) the parts of speech that you know in each sentence in the following order. There are some parts you won't know yet, so don't worry if you leave some blank.

- Write **n** over all of the common nouns and **pn** over all of the proper nouns.
- Write **art** over all of the articles and **adj** over all of the adjectives.
- Write **pro** over all of the pronouns.
- Write **pp** over all of the prepositions.
- Put parentheses around the prepositional phrases.
- Find the verb among the leftover words and mark it with **v**.
- Find the subject that is doing the action in the sentence by asking "Who or what (verb)?" Mark the action verb with **av**.

Then, on a separate sheet of paper, draw a baseline and diagram the subject and verb. If the subject has any modifiers, diagram them. Don't worry about diagramming any of the other words for now. Remember that you can look at your notes if you need help. The example will show you what your answers should look like.

                            pn   av   adj n   pp art   n   pp art adj   adj   n

Example: <u>Mike</u> opened his eyes (in the morning) (after a good, long sleep).

    adj   n   av pro art   adj   n

1) His <u>mom</u> <u>gave</u> him an important job.

     av   adj   n

2) "Clean <u>your</u> room, please!"

   pro av adj   n   n   n

3) He put <u>his</u> clothes, toys, and books away.

     pro   av   adj   n

4) Then <u>he</u> made his bed.

    pro   av   pn   pp adj   n

5) She happily praised Mike (for his <u>effort</u>).

Fill in the blank

6) A sentence must have a _____ and a verb.
   subject

7) A verb expresses physical or _____ action.
   mental

Directions

Write what job each underlined word is doing in each sentence. Choose your answers from the following list:

subject   *object of the preposition*   *verb*   *modifier*

Sentence #	Word	Job
Example	Mike	*subject*
1	gave	*verb*
2	your	*modifier*
3	his	*modifier*
4	he	*subject*
5	effort	*object of the preposition*

5 EXERCISE B

Subject & Verb: Exercise B

Directions
Parse (mark) the parts of speech that you know in each sentence in the following order. There are some parts you won't know yet, so don't worry if you leave some blank.

- Write **n** over all of the common nouns and **pn** over all of the proper nouns.
- Write **art** over all of the articles and **adj** over all of the adjectives.
- Write **pro** over all of the pronouns.
- Write **pp** over all of the prepositions.
- Put parentheses around the prepositional phrases.
- Find the verb among the leftover words and mark it with **v**.
- Find the subject that is doing the action in the sentence by asking "Who or what (verb)?" Mark the action verb with **av**.

Then, on a separate sheet of paper, draw a baseline and diagram the subject and verb. If the subject has any modifiers, diagram them. Don't worry about diagramming any of the other words for now. Remember that you can look at your notes if you need help.

    art   n   pp adj   n   av   art adj   n

1) A family (at our <u>church</u>) bought a new house.

    adj   n   av art n   pp art adj   n   pp adj   n

2) Their son <u>chose</u> a room (on the second floor) (for his bedroom).

    av adj n pp   n   pp adj   n

3) "Put my chest (of drawers) (in <u>this</u> room), please!"

    art   n   pp adj adj   n   av   *   pp art   n   pp art adj adj   n

4) The window (in his new room) <u>opens</u> out (onto the branches) (of a big oak tree).

   *Your student may mark out as a preposition. Remind them that a word is only a preposition if it is in a prepositional phrase.

    art   n   pp adj   n   av adj adj   n

5) The <u>family</u> (from our church) really enjoys their new home.

Fill in the blank

6) A prepositional phrase always ends with a noun or a pronoun called the

    _____.

    object of the preposition

7) If there are words between the preposition and the object of the preposition,

    they are _____.

    modifiers

Directions

Write what job each underlined word is doing in each sentence. Choose your answers from the following list:

subject   **object of the preposition**   **verb**   *modifier*

Sentence #	Word	Job
1	church	*object of the preposition*
2	chose	*verb*
3	this	*modifier*
4	opens	*verb*
5	family	*subject*

5 EXERCISE C

Subject & Verb: Exercise C

Directions
Parse (mark) the parts of speech that you know in each sentence in the following order. There are some parts you won't know yet, so don't worry if you leave some blank.

- Write **n** over all of the common nouns and **pn** over all of the proper nouns.
- Write **art** over all of the articles and **adj** over all of the adjectives.
- Write **pro** over all of the pronouns.
- Write **pp** over all of the prepositions.
- Put parentheses around the prepositional phrases.
- Find the verb among the leftover words and mark it with **v**.
- Find the subject that is doing the action in the sentence by asking "Who or what (verb)?" Mark the action verb with **av**.

Then, on a separate sheet of paper, draw a baseline and diagram the subject and verb. If the subject has any modifiers, diagram them. Don't worry about diagramming any of the other words for now. Remember that you can look at your notes if you need help.

    adj   n   av pro pp adj   n   pp art n   pp art   n
1) My grandfather once told me (about his days) (as a boy) (on the farm).

    pro pp art   n   av   adj   n   pp   art   adj   n
2) All (of the kids) helped their parents (with the farm chores).

       pp art   n   pro   av pp art   n   pp art   n   pp adj   n
3) Early (in the morning), they rushed (to the barn) (for the milking) (of their cows).

    av   adj adj   n
4) Imagine all that work!

    art   n   pp art   n   av adj adj   n   pp   n   pp art   n
5) The members (of the family) did all that work (before school) (in the morning).

Fill in the blank

6) A pronoun is a word that _____.

   takes the place of a noun

7) An adjective is a word that _____.

   modifies a noun or pronoun

Directions

Write what job each underlined word is doing in each sentence. Choose your answers from the following list:

subject   object of the preposition   verb   modifier

Sentence #	Word	Job
1	grandfather	*subject*
2	helped	*verb*
3	their	*modifier*
4	that	*modifier*
5	family	*object of the preposition*

Playing with Words

Verbs are fussy things. You can't just put any old verb with any old subject. For example, we say *I play*, but *he plays*. Sometimes we have to change the verb a little bit when we use it with a different subject.

Now, what if I say this:

    Mr. Contreras **sings** while he **mows** the lawn.

And then say this:

    Mr. Contreras **sang** while he **mowed** the lawn.

When we changed the verbs in the second sentence, what changed about the sentence? Try to explain the difference in your own words:

_____

_____

Fill in the blank in the following sentences, using these verbs. You will use some verbs more than once:

    walk   *walking*   *walks*   *walked*

Earlier today I _____ to school. I usually _____ to school if it's not raining. Yesterday I was _____ to school when my friend said, "Tommy, do you like to _____ to school? I love it!" I said that I love to _____ to school almost as much as he does. He even _____ to school when it's raining!

Now make up some sentences that work together using as many of these verbs as you can:

    makes   *making*   *make*

    made   *eat*   *eats*

    ate   *eating*   *eaten*

If you want to see how you did on these activities, turn to the next page!

Playing with Words
How Did I Do?

After you and your instructor answer these questions about your writing, compare and see if your answers are similar.

Answer the following questions based on your student's work on the previous page. Then compare your answers with your student's.

1) Your words might be different, but here is how changing the verbs changed the sentence:

    The first sentence sounds like it is happening right now. Changing the verbs in the second sentence makes it sound like what Mr. Contreras was doing happened before today.

    This is called changing the verb from the present tense to the past tense. If your answer means the same thing, give yourself two points.

2) Here is what the paragraph should look like with the verbs in the correct places:

    Earlier today I __walked__ to school. I usually __walk__ to school if it's not raining. Yesterday I was __walking__ to school when my friend said, "Tommy, do you like to __walk__ to school? I love it!" I said that I love to __walk__ to school almost as much as he does. He even __walks__ to school when it's raining!

    If you used all of the verbs in the correct places, give yourself 3 points.
    If you made one mistake, give yourself 2 points.
    If you made two mistakes, give yourself 1 point.
    If you made more than two mistakes, give yourself 0 points.

3) Here is how many points to give yourself, depending on how many verbs you were able to correctly use in your sentences:

If you used:	Give yourself:
all 9 verbs	5 points
7 or 8 verbs	4 points
5 or 6 verbs	3 points
3 or 4 verbs	2 points
1 or 2 verbs	1 points

    Now, add up all of your points for your **total points**:

If you got 10 points, you did amazingly!

If you got 9 points, you did incredibly!

If you got 8 points, you did wonderfully!

If you got 7 points, you did a great job.

If you got 6 points, you made a good try.

5 ASSESSMENT

Subject & Verb: Assessment

Directions

Parse (mark) the parts of speech that you know in each sentence in the following order. There are some words you won't know yet, so don't worry if you leave some blank.

- Write **n** over all of the common nouns and **pn** over all of the proper nouns.
- Write **art** over all of the articles and **adj** over all of the adjectives.
- Write **pro** over all of the pronouns.
- Write **pp** over all of the prepositions.
- Put parentheses around the prepositional phrases.
- Find the verb among the leftover words and mark it with **v**.
- Find the subject that is doing the action in the sentence by asking "Who or what (verb)?" Mark the action verb with **av**.

Then, on a separate sheet of paper, draw a baseline and diagram the subject and verb. If the subject has any modifiers, diagram them, too. Remember that you can look at your notes if you need help.

Correctly identified words and prepositional phrases are worth one point each.

        adj   n   pp   adj   n   av   pp art   n

__
11   1) My grandma (on Mom's side) grew up (in the city).

        adj adj   n   av   pp art adj adj   n

__
10   2) Their front door opened (onto a busy city street).

       pp art   n   art   n pp adj   n   av   adj adj   n   pp

__
19   3) (In the afternoon), the kids (in her neighborhood) donned their roller skates (on

       art adj   n

       the front steps).

       av   pp   n   pp art   n

__
8   4) Watch out (for cracks) (in the sidewalk)!

       pn   av   adj   n   pp adj   n   pp art   n

__
12   5) Grandma tells wonderful stories (about her childhood) (in the city).

══
60

Fill in the blank

___ 6) The articles in English are _____ , _____ , and _____ .

3   *a, an, the*

___ 7) Which kind of noun begins with a capital letter? _____

1   *a proper noun*

___ 8) Which kind of noun can only be one word? _____

1   *a common noun*

___ 9) Adjectives are words that

1   _____ .

modify nouns and pronouns

===
6

5 ASSESSMENT

Directions

Write what job each underlined word is doing in each sentence. Choose your answers from the following list:

subject   *object of the preposition*   *verb*   *modifier*

Sentence #	Word	Job
1	grandma	*subject*
2	city	*modifier*
3	kids	*subject*
4	sidewalk	*object of the preposition*
5	tells	*verb*

$\dfrac{}{5}$

Diagrams

Enter score from diagramming solutions here.

$\dfrac{}{16}$

$\dfrac{}{87}$ Total Points $\dfrac{70}{87} = 80\%$

Lesson 6
Adverbs

Instructor Notes

In most cases, if students use The Process, they will find and identify adverbs quite easily. What may give them trouble is figuring out what the adverbs *modify*. Sometimes it's very easy because of the meaning of the word in the sentence. If it's not readily apparent, however, then the concept of "moveability" is handy. **If an adverb can be moved** to more than one place in the sentence without changing the meaning of the sentence or sounding tremendously awkward, **it modifies the verb**. If **it can't be moved** but must stay next to a particular word for the sentence to make sense, **it modifies that word.**

This is also true for prepositional phrases that are doing the adverb job!

Adverbs are tricky, and even experienced grammarians can argue about what they modify. If your student can make an informed argument about why they have diagrammed the adverb or prepositional phrase how they did, give them credit. Then be proud that they are internalizing these grammar lessons!

Diagramming solutions are found at the end of the book.

Lesson 6: Adverbs

Suppose you wanted to say that today you ran around the track in a slow manner. What would you say?

"Today I ran around the track _____."

Whatever word you chose, you have just used another part of speech called an **adverb**. In this sentence, the adverb is a **modifier** that describes *how* you ran around the track. Let's say you chose the word *slowly*. The **adverb** *slowly* modifies the **verb** *ran*. **An adverb can modify a verb.**

Now, what would you say if you wanted to say that today you ran around the track not just *slowly*, but *slowly* to a great degree? What could you say?

"Today I ran around the track _____ slowly."

If you said *very* or *really slowly*, or any other word that tells *how slowly* you ran around the track, guess what? You just used another adverb! Let's say you chose *very*. In this sentence, *very* is an adverb that modifies *slowly*. **An adverb can modify another adverb.**

Okay, what if you blew a big bubblegum bubble that was more than just a *huge* bubble. What word would you put in the blank?

"I blew a(n) _____ huge bubble!"

Did you pick a word like *really*, or *very*, or maybe *unbelievably* or *incredibly*? Yep, you guessed it—whatever word you chose to fill in the blank is an adverb! These adverbs can all be used to tell you *how huge*. *Huge* is an adjective. **An adverb can modify an adjective.**

So, to sum it all up:
An adverb is a word that can modify a verb, an adjective, or another adverb.

The examples all show that adverbs can answer the question "How?" They can also answer the questions "When?", "Where?", or "Why?" Look at the first two examples. Can you find a word that answers the question "When?" That's right; the word ***today*** tells us *when*.

Adverbs that modify verbs can be moved.

As we have been learning, in English, many words have to go in a certain order for the sentence to make sense. That's not true of **adverbs that modify verbs**. You can usually move these adverbs to at least one or two other places in the sentence and it doesn't sound strange or change the meaning of the sentence at all. Let's try it with our first example sentence from above. Remember, there are two adverbs in this sentence: *today* and *slowly*:

Today I ran around the track **slowly**.

I ran around the track **slowly today**.
Slowly today I ran around the track.
I **slowly** ran around the track **today**.
Today I slowly ran around the track.

These four sentences all make sense and mean exactly what the first one means. *Slowly* and *today* both modify the verb *ran*. So if you find a word in a sentence and you think it's an adverb, but you're not sure what it is modifying, try moving it around in the sentence. If you can move it without changing the meaning of the sentence, then you know it must be an adverb that modifies a verb.

What if you try moving it and it doesn't work? Look at the second example above:

Today I ran around the track ***really slowly***.

Can you move *really away* from *slowly* and put it anywhere else in the sentence? No, it doesn't work; it just doesn't make any sense except right where it is. That tells us that, since *really* can't be moved away from *slowly*, it must modify *slowly*. And *slowly* isn't a verb—it's an adverb. You can use the same test on adverbs that modify adjectives. In our third example, if we said an *extremely huge bubble*, we can't move *extremely* away from *huge*.

Diagramming adverbs

Adverbs are diagrammed just like adjectives, on a diagonal line below the baseline. The only difference is that adverbs are attached to verbs, other adverbs, or adjectives. Let's diagram a couple of our example sentences:

Today I ran around the track slowly.

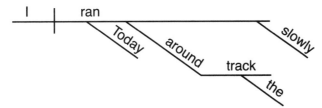

Since the prepositional phrase *around the track* answers the question of **where** I ran, it is acting like an adverb and modifying the verb *ran*. Try moving it around the sentence to check! That's why it is attached to *ran* in the diagram.

Today I ran around the track really slowly.

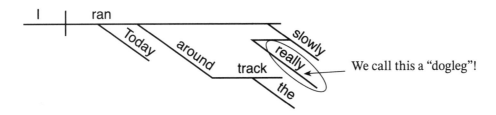

We call this a "dogleg"!

In a sentence where an adverb modifies an adjective or another adverb, use the "dogleg" to attach it to the word it is modifying.

> **Did you notice** that there is no ending punctuation in these diagrams? Most punctuation marks should be left out of diagrams. The only exceptions are apostrophes, some periods (like those after *Mr.* or *Dr.*, for example), and the parentheses around the understood *you* in a command.

A few more handy tips about recognizing adverbs:

- Many adverbs end in *-ly*. In fact, you can change many adjectives (such as *beautiful*) into adverbs by adding *-ly* (*beautifully*).

- The words *not, never, really, very,* and *please* are very commonly used adverbs.

- If you just can't figure out what job a word is doing in a sentence, it's probably an adverb!

Now that you know about adverbs, let's talk a little bit more about diagramming prepositional phrases.

You learned that prepositional phrases are **modifiers**. They can act just like adjectives and tell us "Which boy?" or "Which table?" If a prepositional phrase acts like an adjective and modifies a noun, it's probably located right after the noun it modifies.

```
                art   n   pp art  adj    n    av  art  adj    n
```
Example: The boy (at the next desk) read the whole book.

The prepositional phrase at the *next desk* tells you "Which boy?" It is a modifier for *boy* and should be diagrammed the way you have learned to diagram prepositional phrases: attached to the word *boy*, like this:

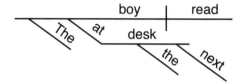

Can you have a prepositional phrase that acts like an adverb? Sure, you can! If there is a prepositional phrase that modifies the verb, it

1) will tell you *how, when, where,* or *why* about that verb, and

2) it can probably be moved around in the sentence, just like a one-word adverb.

When a prepositional phrase modifies an **adjective** or another **adverb**, it

1) tells you *how* about that adjective or adverb, and

2) can't be moved away from that adjective or adverb.

```
     art   n   av   pp    n
```
The boy left (after lunch).

The prepositional phrase after *lunch* tells you *when* the boy *left*. Let's try moving it around in the sentence:

After lunch, the boy left.
The boy, after lunch, left.

Okay, the second sentence is a little weird, but it still makes sense! So you can move *after lunch* around the sentence and it still makes sense. That is one of the clues to identify an adverb that is modifying a verb. Here is how to diagram a prepositional phrase that is doing the adverb job of modifying a verb:

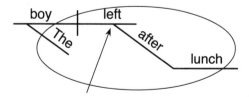

The prepositional phrase is attached to the verb it modifies.

Here is another prepositional phrase doing the adverb job of modifying another adverb:

Example:
```
         pro  av   pro  adv  pp  art   n
         I   called her  later (in  the  day).
```

The word *later* is an adverb, because it says *when* I called. It modifies the verb, and it can be moved around in the sentence. The prepositional phrase tells us *how much* later. Try moving it around the sentence. You can't move *in the day* away from *later*. If you do, it doesn't make sense:

Later, I called her in the day.

So if you want to move the adverb *later*, you need to move its modifier *in the day*, too:

Later (in the day), I called her.
I, later (in the day), called her.

Here is how you should diagram a prepositional phrase that is modifying an adjective or another adverb:

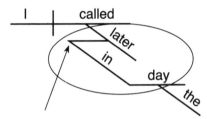

The prepositional phrase is attached to the adverb it modifies with a dogleg.

You can see in the diagram how these two parts of speech, the adverb and the prepositional phrase, are attached. That makes it easy to see that they can't be separated.

Adjectives answer:	**Adverbs answer:**
• *What?*	• *How?*
• *Which?*	• *When?*
• *What kind?*	• *Where?*
	• *Why?*

Adjectives modify:	**Adverbs modify:**
• nouns	• verbs
• pronouns	• adjectives
	• other adverbs.

6 EXERCISE A

Adverbs: Exercise A

Directions

Parse (mark) the parts of speech that you know in each sentence in the following order. There are some parts that you won't know yet, so don't worry if you leave some blank.

- Write **n** over all of the common nouns and **pn** over all of the proper nouns.
- Write **art** over all of the articles and **adj** over all of the adjectives.
- Write **pro** over all of the pronouns.
- Write **pp** over all of the prepositions.
- Put parentheses around the prepositional phrases.
- Find the verb among the leftover words and mark it with **v**.
- Find the subject that is doing the action in the sentence by asking "Who or what (verb)?" Mark the action verb with **av**.
- Mark all of the adverbs with **adv**. Remember that adverbs that modify verbs might be anywhere in the sentence, not always right before or right after the verb!

Then, on a separate sheet of paper, draw a baseline and diagram the subject, verb, and all of their modifiers. Don't worry about diagramming any of the other words for now. If a word has more than one modifier, diagram in the order they appear in the sentence. Remember that you can look at your notes if you need help.

1) (At the high school) (in our town), classes start early.
      pp art adj   n   pp adj   n   n   av   adv

2) (In elementary school), they begin later.
      pp   adj   n   pro   av   adv

3) Today we came (to class) (with our homework).
      adv pro av pp   n   pp   adj   n

4) I always do my homework completely.
      pro adv av adj   n   adv

5) (After school), many students do their homework quickly.
      pp   n   adj   n   av   adj   n   adv

EXERCISE A **6**

Fill in the blank

6) What do we call the noun that a pronoun takes the place of?

   _____
   the antecedent

7) Adverbs are words that modify _____, _____,

   and _____.
   verbs, adjectives, adverbs

8) An adverb that can be moved always modifies the _____.
   verb

Directions

Write what job each underlined word is doing in each sentence. Choose your answers from the following list:

subject　　　　　*object of the preposition*　　　　　*verb*　　　　　*modifier*

Sentence #	Word	Job
1	school	*object of the preposition*
2	begin	*verb*
3	Today	*modifier*
4	my	*modifier*
5	students	*subject*

Adverbs: Exercise B

Directions

Parse (mark) all of the parts of speech that you know. Put parentheses around the prepositional phrases. Then, on a separate piece of paper, diagram the subject, verb, and all of their modifiers. If there are any words left over in the sentence, just ignore them for now. Remember to look at the lesson notes if you need any help!

1) *art adj n adv av adv adv*
   The school day never goes too slowly.

2) *adj adj n pp art n pp n av pp pro adv adv*
   My favorite parts (of the day) (at school) race (by me) so quickly.

3) *art n av adv pp adj n*
   The students work happily (on their projects).

4) *adv art n av adv pp art adv adj n*
   Sometimes, the students mumble grumpily (about the really hard work).

5) *art adj n adv adv av pro art pro*
   The harder work so often teaches us the most.

Short Answer

6) Which kind of noun begins with a capital letter and can consist of more than one word?

   _____.
   a proper noun

Directions

Write what job each underlined word is doing in each sentence. Choose your answers from the following list:

subject *object of the preposition* *verb* *modifier*

Sentence #	Word	Job
1	school	*modifier*
2	day	*object of the preposition*
3	happily	*modifier*
4	hard	*modifier*
5	teaches	*verb*

Adverbs: Exercise C

Directions
Parse all of the parts of speech that you know. Put parentheses around the prepositional phrases. Then, on a separate piece of paper, diagram the subject, verb, and all of their modifiers. If there are any words left over in the sentence, just ignore them for now. Remember to look at the lesson notes if you need any help!

1) The new student peeked nervously (through the classroom door).
   art adj   n   av   adv   pp   art   adj   n

2) Our teacher smiled very happily (at the new boy).
   adj   n   av   adv adv   pp art adj   n

3) She saw his shyness so quickly!
   pro av adj   n   adv adv

4) The teacher spoke really softly (to the other students).
   art   n   av   adv   adv   pp art adj   n

5) "Welcome your new classmate warmly!"
      av   adj adj   n   adv

Fill in the blank

6) The articles in English are _____, _____, and _____.
   a, an, the

7) A proper noun begins with a _____ letter.
   capital

8) (True) or false: If an adverb can't be moved but must stay next to a certain word, it modifies that word.

Exercise C 6

Directions

Write what job each underlined word is doing in each sentence. Choose your answers from the following list:

subject *object of the preposition* *verb* *modifier*

Sentence #	Word	Job
1	student	*subject*
2	smiled	*verb*
3	his	*modifier*
4	students	*object of the preposition*
5	warmly	*modifier*

Playing with Words

Many adverbs are created by adding *-ly* to an adjective. For example, by adding *-ly* to the adjective *quick*, you get the adverb *quickly*. Use the adjective *quick* when you want to modify a noun. Use the adverb *quickly* when you want to modify a verb.

Sarah did a **quick** job of making her bed.
Sarah made her bed **quickly**.

1) Here are some adjectives. Write the adverb form in the space provided by adding *-ly* to each one:

slow _____

beautiful _____

nice _____

careful _____

bad _____

2) Now, put on your creative hat! Write a paragraph using all five of the adverbs that you created. Look at the two sentences about Sarah, above. They might help you come up with ideas for your own sentences.

Playing with Words
How Did I Do?

After you and your instructor answer these questions about your writing, compare and see if your answers are similar.

Answer the following questions based on your student's work on the previous page. Then compare your answers with your student's.

1) The correct answers to this section are:

   slow – slowly
   beautiful – beautifully
   nice – nicely
   careful – carefully
   bad – badly

   Give yourself one point for every one you got right.
   You can get up to five points for this section.

2) If your paragraph makes sense and has

____ adverbs:	Give yourself:
5	5 points
4	4 points
3	3 points
2	2 points
1	1 point

   Add up all of your points to get your **total points:**

If you got 10 points, you did amazingly!

If you got 9 points, you did incredibly!

If you got 8 points, you did wonderfully!

If you got 7 points, you did a great job.

If you got 6 points, you made a good try.

Adverbs: Assessment

Directions

Parse all of the parts of speech that you know. Put parentheses around the prepositional phrases. Then, on a separate piece of paper, diagram the subject, verb, and all of their modifiers. Remember to look at the lesson notes if you need any help!

Each part of speech and prepositional phrase identified correctly is worth one point.

          adj   adv   adj   n   pp art   n   av   pp   pn

__/12   1) My very favorite day (of the week) comes (on Wednesday).

          pp   adj   n   art adj   n   adv   av   adj   n

__/11   2) (On that day), the art teacher regularly visits our classroom.

          pro   adv   av   art adv   adj   n   pp pro

__/10   3) She usually plans a really creative project (for us).

          pro   adv   av   adv   adv   pp   adj   adj   n

__/10   4) I always work so hard (on these fun projects).

          pro adv   av   pp art   n   pp   n   pp   pn

__/13   5) I never wish (for the end) (of school) (on Wednesdays)!

__/56

Fill in the blank

___ **6)** A noun is the name of _____.
1   *a person, place, thing, or idea*

___ **7)** A _____ noun begins with a lowercase letter.
1   *common*

___ **8)** An adjective is a word that _____.
1   *modifies a noun or a pronoun*

___ **9)** A pronoun is a word that _____.
1   *takes the place of a noun*

___ **10)** Adverbs modify _____, _____, and _____.
3   *verbs, adjectives, adverbs*

═══
7

6 ASSESSMENT

Directions

Write what job each underlined word is doing in each sentence. Choose your answers from the following list:

subject   *object of the preposition*   *verb*   *modifier*

Sentence #	Word	Job
1	very	*modifier*
2	teacher	*subject*
3	plans	*verb*
3	us	*object of the preposition*
4	fun	*modifier*
5	I	*subject*

$\dfrac{}{6}$

Diagrams

Enter score from diagramming solutions here.

$\dfrac{}{29}$

$\dfrac{}{98}$ Total Points $\dfrac{78}{98} = 80\%$

Lesson 7
Sentence Patterns 1 & 2

Instructor Notes

This might be a new concept for you, too! It isn't necessary for students to remember what number goes with which pattern. Whenever numbers are mentioned, they are followed by the letters that represent the pattern. If they are not, students should refer to the lesson notes to find the difference. For this lesson, the difference is simple: Pattern 1 doesn't have a direct object, while Pattern 2 does.

In this lesson, students will be introduced to "The Process," which is what we call the structured series of steps that students should follow in order to correctly parse and diagram a sentence. Following The Process makes what seems like a complicated practice into a simple, manageable exercise.

In Step 8 of The Process, the student is to look for a direct object by doing the following:

- say the subject
- say the verb
- ask, "What?"

The answer to this question will be the direct object.

Example: My little brother ate a bug during summer vacation.

The student should parse the sentence (mark all of the different parts of speech that they know: nouns, articles, adjectives, pronouns, prepositions, and verbs). The verb is the action of the sentence; in this case, *ate*. To find the subject, they will say, "Who or what *ate*?" The answer is *brother*. They will then ask, "*brother ate* what?" The answer, of course, is *bug*! *Bug* is the direct object, and the words on the baseline will be, in order, *brother ate bug*.

Diagramming solutions are found at the end of the book.

Lesson 7: Sentence Patterns 1 & 2

Do you know what a **pattern** is? When someone sews a new shirt, they probably use a paper pattern when they cut out the material. They can choose from hundreds and hundreds of fabrics in different colors and designs, but, because they are using a specific pattern, it will still be the same kind of shirt because of how it is put together.

Sentences have patterns, too. Subjects and verbs can only be put together in **five** different patterns in English. Can you believe that? All of the sentences in all of the books *ever written in English*—just five patterns! Just like that shirt that our sewer was making, they can have all kinds of other decorations, but the basic sentence structure must be one of only five.

It's important to understand how these patterns work. In this lesson, you'll learn about the first two sentence patterns and how to recognize them. The patterns are called

    Noun-Verb   and   **Noun-Verb-Noun**

> **Note:** The *N* in sentence patterns can stand for either **noun** or **pronoun**.

Pattern 1: Noun-Verb (N-V)

The noun-verb pattern (which we'll call N-V from now on) contains only two items on the baseline of the diagram: the subject, which is a noun or pronoun (**N**), and an action verb (**V**). The subject and verb may have modifiers (articles, adjectives, and prepositional phrases modifying the subject; and adverbs and prepositional phrases modifying the verb), but there are **no other nouns or verbs** that go on the baseline of the diagram.

                  art   n   av   pp art   adj   n

Example: The boy stood (on the baseball field).

You already know how to diagram this kind of sentence:

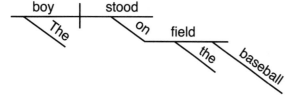

There are only two things on the baseline: the subject *boy* and the verb *stood*. Everything else in the sentence is a modifier (or part of a modifier) for one of those two words.

Pattern 2: Noun-Verb-Noun (N-V-N)

To learn about the Noun-Verb-Noun (N-V-N) pattern, you need to know about a new "job" that a noun can do, called the ***direct object***. A direct object is a noun or pronoun that is receiving the action of the verb, or having the action done to it. It answers the question, "(subject) (verb) what?" When you take all of the modifiers out of a sentence in this pattern, you are left with **three** items on the baseline: the subject (**N**), the verb (**V**) and another noun (**N**), which is the direct object. There may be modifiers for all three of these parts, but there are **no other nouns or verbs** on the baseline.

To find the direct object, first find the subject and verb. You already know how to do that!

- Parse the sentence (mark all of the words you can identify).

    adj adj   n   av art   adj   n   adv
    My best friend had a birthday party today.

- Strip the sentence of all of its modifiers.

    ~~adj~~ ~~adj~~   n   av ~~art~~ ~~adj~~   n   ~~adv~~
    ~~My~~ ~~best~~ friend had ~~a~~ ~~birthday~~ party ~~today~~.

    All that is left is *friend had party*. That means the pattern is noun-verb-noun (N-V-N).

- Go ahead and draw the baseline, then find the subject and verb and write them in:

- Plug these into your question "(subject) (verb) what?" Try it: "friend had *what*?" The answer is "friend had **party**." ***Party*** is the direct object.

Here's how the direct object should be diagrammed:

Notice that the line between the verb and the direct object goes to the baseline and then **stops.**

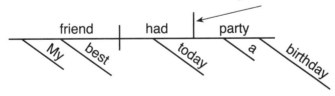

To help you make sure you can identify and diagram all of the parts of the sentence, we have something we call "The Process." If you go through each step in order, it will make things very easy for you. You have already been doing everything up to step 8, identifying and marking all of the parts of speech in a specific order! Give it a try on the next exercise.

Remember, if you just can't figure out what job a word is doing in a sentence, it's probably an adverb!

7 STUDENT NOTES

The Process

Step 1: Find all of the nouns in the sentence and mark them with either *n* (for common nouns) or *pn* (for proper nouns).

Step 2: Find and mark all articles (*art*) and adjectives (*adj*) by asking, "Which (noun)?"

Step 3: Find and mark all of the pronouns with *pro*.

Step 4: Find all of the prepositions and mark them with *pp*. Put parentheses around the prepositional phrases.

Step 5: Find all of the verbs and mark them with *v*.

Step 6: Find the subject by answering the question, "Who or what (verb)?"

Step 7: Draw the baseline and fill in the subject and verb.

Step 8: Look for a direct object. Say the subject and verb, and ask, "What?"

If there is no answer:

This is a Pattern 1 (N-V) sentence. The baseline is done. It looks like this:

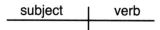

Write *a* in front of the *v* you already wrote over the verb.

If there is an answer:

This is a Pattern 2 (N-V-N) sentence. The baseline looks like this:

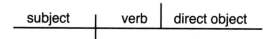

Write *a* in front of the *v* you already wrote over the verb. Write the direct object on the baseline.

Step 9: Add all of the modifiers.

Sentence Patterns 1 & 2: Exercise A

Directions

All of the sentences below are Pattern 2, so you know they have a direct object. Parse (mark) all of the parts of speech and put parentheses around the prepositional phrases. Then diagram the entire sentence. Use "The Process" in your notes to help you.

    pro av adj adj   n   pp art   n   pp art adj   adj   n

1) I met my best <u>friend</u> (at the park) (on a warm summer day).

    pro   av   art   n   pp   n   pp   adj   n

2) <u>We</u> played a game (of hopscotch) (with other kids).

    art   n   pp art adj   n   adv   av   art   n

3) A girl (in a <u>red</u> t-shirt) shyly made a request.

    adv   av   pro pp art   n

4) "Please let me (in the <u>game</u>)."

    art   n   pp art   n   av   pro

5) The kids (in the game) <u>welcomed</u> her.

Fill in the blank

6) Pronouns are words that _____ .
     take the place of nouns

7) To find the direct object, say the _____ , say the _____ ,

and ask _____ .
   subject, verb, "what?"

7 EXERCISE A

Directions
Write what job the underlined words are doing in each sentence. Choose your answers from the following list:

subject   object of the preposition   verb   modifier   direct object

Sentence #	Word	Job
1	friend	*direct object*
2	We	*subject*
3	red	*modifier*
4	game	*object of the preposition*
5	welcomed	*verb*

Sentence Patterns 1 & 2: Exercise B

Directions

The sentences below may be either Pattern 1 or Pattern 2. Parse (mark) all of the parts of speech and put parentheses around the prepositional phrases. Then diagram the entire sentence.
Use "The Process" in your notes to help you figure out if the sentence is Pattern 1 or Pattern 2.

     adj adj   n   av   pp art   n   pp adj   n

1) My best friend <u>lives</u> (in a house) (on my block).

    pro av pro pp art   n   pp   n

2) I meet <u>him</u> (at the corner) (after school).

     adv   pro av adj   n   pp   art   n

3) Sometimes, we ride <u>our</u> bikes (around the neighborhood).

    adv   pro av pp adv*   adj   n

4) Today, we rode (to another friend's <u>house</u>).

*If your student marks another *as an adjective, help them to see that the house belongs to* another friend, *so* another *is modifying* friend's. *The phrase* friend's another house *doesn't make sense, because both words aren't modifying* house.

    pro   av art adj   n   pp adj   n   pp art adj   n

5) <u>We</u> played a little game (of touch football) (in the front yard).

Fill in the blank

6) An adjective is a word that _____.
       modifies a noun or a pronoun

7) In a prepositional phrase, the last word is the _____.
       object of the preposition

7 EXERCISE B

Directions
Write what job the underlined words are doing in each sentence. Choose your answers from the following list:

subject   *object of the preposition*   *verb*   *modifier*   *direct object*

Sentence #	Word	Job
1	lives	*verb*
2	him	*direct object*
3	our	*modifier*
4	house	*object of the preposition*
5	We	*subject*

Sentence Patterns 1 & 2: Exercise C

Directions

The sentences below may be either Pattern 1 or Pattern 2. Parse (mark) all of the parts of speech and put parentheses around the prepositional phrases. Then diagram the entire sentence.
Use "The Process" in your notes to help you figure out if the sentence is Pattern 1 or Pattern 2.

pro   av   art adv   adj   n   pp   adj   n

1) I remember a really great day (during winter break).

pro av adj adj   n   pp art   adj   n

2) I met my best friend (at the shopping mall).

pro   av   adv   pp   n   pp adj   n

3) We shopped together (for presents) (for our parents).

adv pro av   n   pp art adj   n

4) Then we ate lunch (at the food court).

pro   adv   av art adj   n   adv

5) We certainly had a terrific day together.

6) **Circle the word or words that could NOT be a modifier.**

   prepositional phrase   article   (direct object)   adjective

Fill in the blank

7) Pattern 2 is just like Pattern 1 except it has a _____.
   direct object

7 Exercise C

Directions
Write what job each underlined word is doing in each sentence. Choose your answers from the following list:

subject *object of the preposition* *verb* *modifier* *direct object*

Sentence #	Word	Job
1	I	*subject*
2	met	*verb*
3	parents	*object of the preposition*
4	lunch	*direct object*
5	certainly	*modifier*

Playing with Words

Can you write a Pattern 1 (N-V) sentence using the nouns *daisy* and *arrow*? How about this one:

The *arrow* went into the center of the *daisy*.

Arrow is the subject (N) and *went* is the verb (V). *Daisy* is the object of the preposition.

Now, can you write a Pattern 2 (N-V-N) sentence using the nouns *daisy* and *arrow*? Here's one:

***Daisy* shot an *arrow* at the target.**

Daisy is a proper noun that is the subject (N), *shot* is the verb (V), and *arrow* is the direct object (N).

Now you try! Don't worry if your sentences seem silly, as long as they follow in the patterns.

1) Write a Pattern 1 (N-V) sentence using the nouns *carpet* and *cat*.

_____

_____

2) Now write a Pattern 2 (N-V-N) sentence using the same two nouns, *carpet* and *cat*.

_____

_____

3) Here is a list of nouns and pronouns. On a separate piece of paper, use as many of these nouns or pronouns as you can to write three sentences that work together in a paragraph. One of the sentences needs to be Pattern 1 and another needs to be Pattern 2. The third sentence can be either pattern.

| *paper* | *book* | *student* | *Tom* | *he* | *it* |
| *Mom* | *girl* | *homework* | *she* | *milk* | *pie* |

Now look at the following page to see how you did!

Playing with Words
How Did I Do?

After you and your instructor answer these questions about your writing, compare and see if your answers are similar.

Answer the following questions based on your student's work on the previous page. Then compare your answers with your student's.

1) Did you use both nouns? If you did, give yourself one point. _____

Did you write a Pattern 1 (N-V) sentence?
If yes, give yourself one point. _____

2) Did you use both nouns? If you did, give yourself one point. _____

Did you write a Pattern 2 (N-V-N) sentence?
If yes, give yourself one point. _____

3) Does your paragraph have at least three sentences?
If it does, give yourself two points. _____

How many words from the list did you use? _____

If you used:	Give yourself:
12 words	4 points
9–11 words	3 points
6–8 words	2 points
1–5 words	1 point

Now add up all of your points to get your **total points:** ══════════

If you got 10 points, you did amazingly!

If you got 9 points, you did incredibly!

If you got 8 points, you did wonderfully!

If you got 7 points, you did a great job.

If you got 6 points, you made a good try.

Sentence Patterns 1 & 2: Assessment

Directions

The sentences below may be either Pattern 1 or Pattern 2. Parse (mark) all of the parts of speech and put parentheses around the prepositional phrases. Then diagram the entire sentence.
Use "The Process" from your notes to help you figure out if the sentence is Pattern 1 or Pattern 2.

Each part of speech and prepositional phrase identified correctly is worth one point.

         pn   av adj adj   n   pp   art adj   n

__10__ 1) Jeannie liked her best friend (from the very beginning).

        pro   av pp ———adj——— n   pp   n

__9__ 2) They met (in Mrs. Wilson's class) (at school)!

       art adj   n   adv   av art n   adv   pp   pn

__11__ 3) The two girls always spent the day together (on Saturdays).

      pro adv av pp art adj   n   pp   pn

__11__ 4) They even went (to the same church) (on Sundays).

       pn   av   adj   n   pp   pn

__7__ 5) Jeannie treasured her friendship (with Sofia).

__48__

7 ASSESSMENT

Fill in the blank

___ 6) The articles in English are _____, _____, and _____.
3   *a, an, the*

___ 7) A noun is the name of a _____, _____, _____, or _____.
4   *person, place, thing, idea*

___ 8) The baseline of a Pattern 2 sentence contains the _____,
3   _____, and _____.

    subject, verb, direct object

___ 9) _____ go on a slanted line attached to the word they modify.
1   *Modifiers*

==
11

ASSESSMENT 7

Directions

Write what job each underlined word is doing in each sentence. Choose your answers from the following list:

subject *object of the preposition* *verb* *modifier* *direct object*

Each correct answer is worth one point.

Sentence #	Word	Job
1	her	*modifier*
2	class	*object of the preposition*
3	girls	*subject*
4	went	*verb*
5	friendship	*direct object*

$$\frac{}{5}$$

Diagrams

Enter score from diagramming solutions here.

$$\frac{}{32}$$

$$\frac{}{96} \text{ Total Points} \quad \frac{77}{96} = 80\%$$

Lesson 8
Sentence Pattern 3

Instructor Notes

A Pattern 3 sentence is just like a Pattern 2 sentence, but with the addition of an indirect object. In this lesson, students will learn a helpful trick that we call "undecorating" the sentence. That means that, after parsing the sentence, the students mentally (or physically; they could lightly cross words out with pencil, if it's helpful for them) take out all of the modifiers: articles, adjectives, prepositional phrases, and adverbs. What they have left will be the baseline of their diagram. If what's left over is noun-verb, they have a Pattern 1 sentence. If they have noun-verb-noun left, they have Pattern 2. If they have noun-verb-noun-noun, it's Pattern 3, which they will learn about in this lesson.

Remind them that if the sentence is a command, the subject will be an "understood" *you*, so it's not visible, but it's still there. They write it on their diagram like this: (you).

Diagramming solutions are found at the end of the book.

Sentence Patterns 3

In this lesson, you will learn about a new sentence pattern. You're also going to learn about a useful trick that will really help you with your diagramming! We call the trick "undecorating the sentence."

How (and why) to undecorate a sentence

The words that go on the baseline of a sentence diagram are the really important words in the sentence. If you didn't have those words, you wouldn't have a sentence! So the words on the baseline are definitely **not** the decorations of a sentence.

Now, think about all of the modifiers that you know—the articles, adjectives, adverbs, and prepositional phrases—which are diagrammed below the baseline. You can take all of them away, and you would still have a sentence. It won't be as interesting, and it might sound a little odd, but it's still a sentence.

Here's the trick: parse (mark) all of the parts of speech in the sentence, and put parentheses around the prepositional phrases. Then **remove all of the modifiers**, or decorations, from the sentence. You can do this in your head, or you can cross things out with your pencil. After you've done that, look at what you have left. The remaining words are all words that go on the baseline! Try it with some of the sentences in Lesson 7. It works well, doesn't it?

Having a trick like this is going to be very helpful for you as we continue to learn about more complicated sentences and grammar guidelines.

Sentence Pattern 3 (N-V-N-N)

This sentence pattern is called **noun-verb-noun-noun**. To understand it, you will need to know about another job that nouns and pronouns can do called an **indirect object**. You know that the subject is the noun or pronoun that *does* the action of an action verb, and the direct object is the noun or pronoun that the action is *done to*. The indirect object is a noun or pronoun that is *affected by*, or *receiving the result of*, the action.

                pn   av   pro art   n   pp   n

Example: Mom gave me a dollar (for candy).

If we undecorate the sentence, what do we have left? After removing any modifiers, we are left with:

              n   v   pro   n

Mom gave me dollar

Mom is the subject. **Mom** is doing the action.

Gave is the verb. **Gave** is the action that is being done.

Dollar is the direct object. **Dollar** is what the action is done to: the dollar is the thing being given.

Me is affected by the action. **Me** is receiving the result of the action: the dollar is given to **me**.

Now, let's look at those words again:

Mom gave me dollar

These words, in this order, show what the baseline should look like:

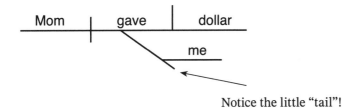

Notice the little "tail"!

The indirect object hangs below the verb. The diagonal line has a little tail that goes past the horizontal line.

Remember: The words in a Pattern 3 (N-V-N-N) sentence **always** come in the same order: **subject – action verb – indirect object – direct object.**

Let's try another one that's a little more tricky (don't worry, you'll get it!):

   adv   av   pro art n
   Please write me a letter.

If we undecorate this sentence, here's what we have left:

   av   pro   n
   write me letter

Hmm. We have a verb followed by two nouns (even though one is a pronoun, you can still think of it as a noun). So what is going on?

Did you remember? This sentence is a command, so it **does** have another noun: the understood *you*! That means that what we really have left is:

   pro   av   pro   n
   (you) write me letter

There it is: our N-V-N-N pattern that tells us that this is a Pattern 3 sentence, so it includes an indirect object!

N	V	N	N
subject	*action verb*	*indirect object*	*direct object*
(you)	write	me	letter

Here's how you would diagram the whole sentence (including the modifiers):

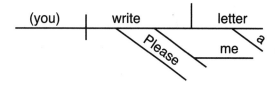

EXERCISE A **8**

Sentence Patterns 3: Exercise A

Directions

All of the sentences below are Sentence Pattern 3 (N-V-N-N). Parse (mark) all of the parts of speech and put parentheses around the prepositional phrases. Then diagram the entire sentence. Remember to use all of your tools if you need any help:

- Use The Process (in Lesson 7 notes).
- Undecorate the sentence.
- Look back at the lesson notes.

    adj   n   av pro art   adj   n pp art   n

1) My uncle gave me an important job (at the airport).

    av pro art   n   pp   adj   n

2) "Send me a postcard (from your trip)."

   pro av   pro art   n   pp   pro

3) I made myself a promise (about that).

  pp art adj   n pp adj   n   adj   n   av pro art   n

4) (On the third day) (of our trip), my mom handed me a postcard.

    av   adj   n   art adj   n   adv

5) "Write your uncle a little note, please."

Fill in the blank

6) The last word in a prepositional phrase is called the

_____ .

  object of the preposition

7) The articles in English are _____, _____, and _____.
    a, an, the

8 EXERCISE A

Directions
Write what job the underlined words are doing in each sentence. Choose your answers from the following list:

subject	*object of the preposition*	*verb*
modifier	*direct object*	*indirect object*

Sentence #	Word	Job
1	My	*modifier*
2	Send	*verb*
3	myself	*indirect object*
4	mom	*subject*
4	postcard	*direct object*
5	uncle	*indirect object*

Sentence Patterns 3: Exercise B

Directions

All of the sentences below are either Pattern 2 (N-V-N) or Pattern 3 (N-V-N-N). Parse all of the parts of speech and put parentheses around the prepositional phrases. Then diagram the entire sentence. Remember to undecorate the sentence, use The Process, and look back at the lesson notes if you need any help.

pro av n pp n pp adj n

1) I send <u>lots</u> (of cards) (to my relatives).

adj n av pro n pp adj n

2) Some people send <u>others</u> cards (on special occasions).

art adj n av adj n pp n

3) The <u>card</u> companies create all sorts (of cards).

adj n av n art adj n pp adj n

4) Funny cards <u>give</u> people a real lift (in hard times).

av adj adj n pp n

5) Remember your loved ones (with <u>cards</u>).

Fill in the blank

6) An adverb that can be moved modifies the _____.
   verb

7) A Pattern 2 sentence has a subject, a verb, and a _____.
   direct object

8 EXERCISE B

Directions

Write what job the underlined words are doing in each sentence. Choose your answers from the following list:

subject   *object of the preposition*   *verb*
modifier   *direct object*   *indirect object*

Sentence #	Word	Job
1	lots	*direct object*
2	others	*indirect object*
3	card	*modifier*
4	give	*verb*
5	cards	*object of the preposition*

Sentence Patterns 3: Exercise C

Directions

The sentences below could be Pattern 1 (N-V), Pattern 2 (N-V-N), or Pattern 3 (N-V-N-N). Parse all of the parts of speech and put parentheses around the prepositional phrases. Then diagram the entire sentence. Remember to undecorate the sentence, use The Process, and look back at the lesson notes if you need any help.

adj   n   pp   n   av   pp pro   pp   art   n   pp   pn
1) My sister (in <u>college</u>) talks (to us) (on the phone) (on Sundays).

adv   pro   av   pro art   adj   n   pp   art   adj   n
2) Sometimes, <u>she</u> sends us a funny card (from the college bookstore).

adj   n   av   n   pp   n   pp pro
3) My mom <u>prepares</u> packages (of goodies) (for her).

adj   n   adv   av   adj   n
4) My sister really loves those <u>packages</u>.

av   pro   adj   n   adv   adv
5) "Send <u>me</u> another package soon, please!"

Fill in the blank

6) When you undecorate a sentence, you take out all of the _____.
   modifiers

7) If you undecorate a Pattern 3 (N-V-N-N) sentence, there are four main parts left.

   They are (in order): _____, _____,

   _____, _____.
   subject, action verb, indirect object, direct object

8 Playing with Words

Directions

Write what job each underlined word is doing in each sentence. Choose your answers from the following list:

subject   *object of the preposition*   *verb*

modifier   *direct object*   *indirect object*

Sentence #	Word	Job
1	college	*object of the preposition*
2	she	*subject*
3	prepares	*verb*
4	packages	*direct object*
5	me	*indirect object*

Playing with Words

Here are three nouns.

Tim **sandwich** **table**

We're going to use these three nouns in three kinds of sentences: one Pattern 1 (N-V), one Pattern 2 (N-V-N), and one Pattern 3 (N-V-N-N). Here's what we came up with:

Pattern 1: **Tim** played with his **sandwich** at the **table**.
Pattern 2: **Tim** put the **sandwich** on the **table**.
Pattern 3: His mom made **Tim** the **sandwich** on the **table**.

The way we did this was to put at least one of the nouns in a modifier (here, prepositional phrases), so that when we undecorate it, we are left with the pattern we were looking for.

Now you try! Here are your three nouns:

brother **dad** **book**

Hint: If you're not sure you have the right pattern, undecorate your sentence to see!

1) Pattern 1 (N-V):

_____

_____

2) Pattern 2 (N-V-N):

_____

_____

3) Pattern 3 (N-V-N-N):

_____

_____

8 PLAYING WITH WORDS

4) Here's another challenge—we know you can do it! Write a sentence that has these parts of speech in this order:

    art   *adj*   *n*   *pp*   *art*   *n*   *av*   *pn*   *art*   *n*

                    art *adj* *n*   *pp* *art* *n*   *av* *pn* *art* *n*
Example: The old lady from the city gave Mary a gift.

Now you try!

    art   *adj*   *n*   *pp*   *art*   *n*   *av*   *pn*   *art*   *n*

_____

Playing with Words
How Did I Do?

After you and your instructor answer these questions about your writing, compare and see if your answers are similar.

Answer the following questions based on your student's work on the previous page. Then compare your answers with your student's.

1) Did you use all three nouns? Give yourself one point. _____

   Is your sentence a N-V sentence? Give yourself one point. _____

2) Did you use all three nouns? Give yourself one point. _____

   Is your sentence a N-V-N sentence? Give yourself one point. _____

3) Did you use all three nouns? Give yourself one point. _____

   Is your sentence a N-V-N-N sentence? Give yourself one point. _____

4) Parse the sentence. How many parts of speech do you have in the right order? _____

If you have:	Give yourself:
10 words	4 points
8–9 words	3 points
6–7 words	2 points
4–5 words	1 point
fewer than 4 words	0 points

Now, add up all of your points for your **total points!** ════════════

If you got 10 points, you did amazingly!

If you got 9 points, you did incredibly!

If you got 8 points, you did wonderfully!

If you got 7 points, you did a great job.

If you got 6 points, you made a good try.

8 Assessment

Sentence Patterns 3: Assessment

Directions

The sentences below could be Pattern 1 (N-V), Pattern 2 (N-V-N), or Pattern 3 (N-V-N-N). Parse all of the parts of speech and put parentheses around the prepositional phrases. Then diagram the entire sentence. Remember to undecorate the sentence, use The Process, and look back at the lesson notes if you need any help.

$\frac{\quad}{10}$ 1)   *adj*   *n*   *av*   *pp*   *n*   *pp*   *art*   *n*
Some children go (to camp) (in the summer).

$\frac{\quad}{9}$ 2)   *pro*   *adv*   *av*   *adj*   *n*   *pp*   *art*   *n*
They often miss their families (for a while).

$\frac{\quad}{11}$ 3)   *adv*   *art*   *adj*   *n*   *av*   *adj*   *n*   *art*   *adj*   *adj*   *n*
Sometimes, a homesick kid writes their parents a sad little note.

$\frac{\quad}{7}$ 4)   *adv*   *av*   *pro*   *pp*   *adj*   *n*
"Please rescue me (from this place)!"

$\frac{\quad}{13}$ 5)   *pp*   *art*   *adj*   *n*   *n*   *av*   *art*   *adj*   *n*   *pp*   *n*
(Within a few days), kids have a great time (at camp).

$\frac{\overline{\quad}}{50}$

ASSESSMENT **8**

Short answer
Each correct answer is worth one point.

___ **6)** A Pattern 3 sentence is just like a Pattern 2 sentence, except that it has a(n)
 1
  _____.

  indirect object

___ **7)** A sentence which is a command usually has _____
 1
  as a subject.

  an understood "you"

___ **8)** In a Pattern 3 (N-V-N-N) sentence, which N represents the direct object: the first, the second,
 1
  or the third? _____

  the third

___ **9)** True or (False) : A proper noun begins with a lowercase letter. (Circle your answer.)
 1

===
 4

8 ASSESSMENT

Directions

Write what job the underlined words are doing in each sentence. Choose your answers from the following list:

subject   *object of the preposition*   *verb*

modifier   *direct object*   *indirect object*

Each correct answer is worth one point.

Sentence #	Word	Job
1	go	*verb*
2	They	*subject*
2	their	*modifier*
3	Sometimes	*modifier*
3	parents	*indirect object*
4	me	*direct object*
5	days	*object of the preposition*

$\overline{\overline{7}}$

Diagrams

Enter score from diagramming solutions here.

$\overline{\overline{38}}$

$\overline{\overline{99}}$ Total Points $\dfrac{79}{99} = 80\%$

Lesson 9
Linking Verbs and Sentence Patterns 4 & 5

Instructor Notes

What could make this lesson exciting and fun is that students are ready to use the complete Process Chart that they've been building for several lessons. This type of orderly, sequential thinking might be new for your student, but it's an extremely valuable skill for them to acquaint themselves with, since it can (and will!) be useful to them in many different disciplines throughout their lives. It's the kind of thought process needed to do higher-level math and science, and use other higher-order thinking skills. It might be a good idea for you to work through the first one or two sentences of each exercise with your student so that they can become comfortable with the Process Chart. Once they realize how easily and consistently the chart works—how it neatly shows them how to diagram any sentence—they will quickly become adept at using it.

Diagramming solutions are found at the back of the book.

Lesson 9: Linking Verbs and Sentence Patterns 4 & 5

Look at this sentence:

> James walked down the street.

The subject of this sentence is *James*. And James **did** something in the sentence: he **walked**.

Now, look at this sentence:

> James seemed sleepy today.

The subject is still *James*, but James isn't **doing** anything in this sentence. Instead, he is **being** something: *sleepy*.

Here are two more sentences to look at. In which one is the subject **doing** something, and in which is the subject **being** something?

> The girl tasted the batter.   The batter tasted sweet.

In the first sentence, the subject (*girl*) is **doing** something: she's *tasting*. In the second, the subject (*batter*) isn't tasting anything. It's **being** something: *sweet!*

Sentences where the subjects are **doing** something have **action verbs**. But sentences where the subjects are **being** something have **linking verbs**. They are called **linking verbs** because they **link** the subject with either another name for the subject or an adjective that describes it.

Not every verb can be a linking verb. Here is a list of some common verbs that can be linking verbs:

be (am, is, are, was, were, being, been)	look
seem	taste
become	feel
appear	smell
stay	grow
remain	sound

Predicate

We know that, in order to have a sentence, there must be a **subject** and a **verb**. There's another way that sentences can be divided: subject and **predicate**. The **predicate** includes the verb, but also anything else that isn't the subject or the subject's modifiers. The terms you will learn for Sentence Patterns 4 and 5 include the word **predicate**, because they are not parts of the subject, and they follow the verb. They are in the **predicate** of the sentence.

subject	predicate
James	walked down the street.
James	seemed sleepy today.
The girl	tasted the batter.
The batter	tasted sweet.

Linking verbs connect **complements** to the subject. A **complement** is something that completes another thing or makes it better. There are two kinds of complements: **predicate nominatives** and **predicate adjectives.**

Sentence Pattern 4 (N-LV-N):
This pattern is called **noun-linking verb-noun**. The baseline items come in this order:
subject (noun or pronoun) - **linking verb** - **predicate nominative** (another noun or pronoun).

A **predicate nominative** is a noun or pronoun that is another word for the subject that follows a linking verb. It is a **complement** of the subject.

                        adj adj   n   lv art adj   n
Example: My big brother is an eighth grader.

First, strip away all of the modifiers. Here's what we have left:

     n   lv   n
brother is grader

We could also find the subject and verb, then ask the question, "brother is **what**?" We get the same answer: **brother is grader**. Are **brother** and **grader** the same person? Yes, in this sentence, they are. That means we have a **N-LV-N** sentence and **grader** is the **predicate nominative**. **Grader** is another word that means the same person as the subject **brother**. The person described in this sentence is a big brother and also an eighth grader. The verb *is* links these two names together.

Here's how to diagram a N-LV-N sentence:

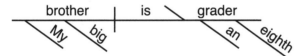

The predicate nominative goes on the baseline after the subject and the verb. Can you see how this diagram is different from a sentence with a direct object? Yes, the line between the verb (*is*) and the predicate nominative (*grader*) is slanted toward the subject (*brother*).

Sentence Pattern 5 (N-LV-ADJ):
Sometimes the subject is linked to a modifier that describes it. That modifier is called a **predicate adjective**.

A **predicate adjective** is an adjective that follows a linking verb and describes the subject. It is a **complement** to the subject.

The words on the baseline are in this order:
subject (noun or pronoun) – **linking verb** – **predicate adjective**.

Here's an example:

                        art   n   lv   adj   pp   art adj   n
Example: The students were happy (about the field trip).

To find the sentence pattern, identify the subject (**students**) and the verb (**were**), then ask yourself, "*students* were **what**?" The answer is: **students were happy**. The adjective **happy** describes the subject **students**. That means that we have a **N-LV-ADJ** sentence: **students** (N) – **were** (LV) – **happy** (ADJ).

Sentence Pattern 5 is diagrammed the same way as Sentence Pattern 4:

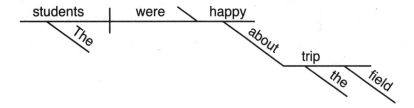

The predicate adjective (***happy***) goes on the baseline after the verb. It is separated from the linking verb (***were***) with a slanted line pointing back to the subject (***students***).

Remember:

- If you have an **action verb** in your sentence, then it must be Pattern 1, Pattern 2, or Pattern 3.

- If you have a **linking verb**, it must be either Pattern 4 or Pattern 5. The linking verb links the subject to the **complement**: either the predicate nominative (they are the same person or thing) or the predicate adjective (describing the subject).

On the next page is the now-complete Process Chart. It might look scary, but you know how to do everything it shows! Just follow each step and answer the questions in order, and you will see how easy it is to recognize sentence patterns and parts of speech!

The Process

Step 1: Find all of the nouns in the sentence and mark them with either *n* (for common nouns) or *pn* (for proper nouns).

Step 2: Find and mark all articles (*art*) and adjectives (*adj*) by asking, "Which (noun)?"

Step 3: Find and mark all of the pronouns with *pro*.

Step 4: Find all of the prepositions and mark them with *pp*. Put parentheses around the prepositional phrases.

Step 5: Find all of the verbs and mark them with *v*.

Step 6: Find the subject by answering the question, "Who or what (verb)?"

Step 7: Draw the baseline and fill in the subject and verb.

Step 8: Look for a direct object. Say the subject and verb, and ask, "What?"

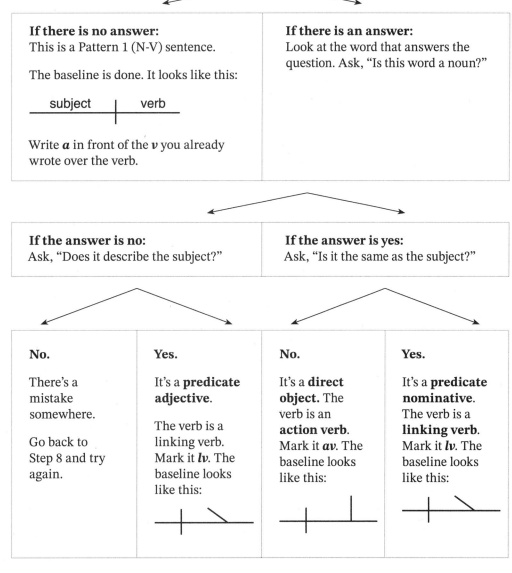

Step 9: Add all of the modifiers.

Step 10: Congratulate yourself! You've successfully parsed and diagrammed the whole sentence!

9 EXERCISE A

Linking Verbs and Sentence Patterns 4 & 5: Exercise A

Directions

All of the sentences below are Pattern 4 (N-LV-N). Parse all of the parts of speech and put parentheses around the prepositional phrases. Then diagram each sentence. Be sure to use The Process Chart and the lesson notes if you need help.

    adj   n   lv   n   pp art   n

1) Most pets are part (of the family).

    n   adv   lv   n   pp art   n

2) Dogs usually become members (of the family).

    adj adj   n   lv art adj   adj   n

3) My favorite dog was a beautiful brown collie.

   pp adj   n   adj   n   lv adj adj   n

4) (In my mind), that dog was my big sister.

   pro lv adj   n   pp   n   pp   n

5) She was my protector (in case) (of danger)!

Fill in the blank

6) In a noun-linking verb-noun sentence, the second noun is called the

_____.

predicate nominative

7) The word at the end of a prepositional phrase is called the

_____.

object of the preposition

Exercise A 9

Directions

Write what job the underlined words are doing in each sentence. Choose your answers from the following list:

subject *object of the preposition* *verb*
modifier *predicate nominative* *predicate adjective*

Sentence #	Word	Job
1	pets	*subject*
2	usually	*modifier*
3	was	*verb*
4	sister	*predicate nominative*
5	case	*object of the preposition*

9 EXERCISE B

Linking Verbs and Sentence Patterns 4 & 5: Exercise B

Directions
The sentences below may be either Pattern 4 (N-LV-N) or Pattern 5 (N-LV-ADJ). Parse all of the parts of speech and put parentheses around the prepositional phrases. Then diagram each sentence. Be sure to use The Process Chart and the lesson notes if you need help.

    adj   adj   n   lv   pn

1) My collie's name was Jenny.

    adj   adj   adj   n   lv   adj

2) Her thick brown fur was beautiful.

   pn   lv   adv   adj

3) Jenny was really smart.

   adj   n   lv   adv   adj

4) Her tricks were very clever!

   pn   lv   art adj n   pp adj   n

5) Jenny was a big part (of our lives).

Fill in the blank

6) A noun that begins with a lowercase letter and only consists of one word is a

   _____ noun.
   common

7) Adverbs modify _____, _____,

   and _____.
   verbs, adjectives, adverbs

Exercise B 9

Directions

Write what job the underlined words are doing in each sentence. Choose your answers from the following list:

subject *object of the preposition* *verb*
modifier *predicate nominative* *predicate adjective*

Sentence #	Word	Job
1	Jenny	*predicate nominative*
2	beautiful	*predicate adjective*
3	Jenny	*subject*
4	were	*verb*
5	our	*modifier*

9 EXERCISE C

Linking Verbs and Sentence Patterns 4 & 5: Exercise C

Directions
The sentences below may be any of the five sentence patterns. Parse all of the parts of speech and put parentheses around the prepositional phrases. Then diagram each sentence. Remember to use The Process Chart! You can also look at the lesson notes if you need help.

    pp   adj   n   pn av adj adj n
1) (During dinner time), Jenny did her best tricks.

    adj adj   n   lv art n   pp art adj   n
2) Her main goal was a treat (from the dinner table).

    pro av adv* pp art adv adj   n
3) She sat up (in a very funny position).

*Remind your student that a word can only be a preposition if it is in a prepositional phrase. Up is an adverb modifying sat.

    pro av pro art adj   n   pp adj adj adj   n
4) She gave us a sad look (from her big brown eyes).

    adj   n   lv   adv   adj
5) Her tricks were usually successful!

Fill in the blank

6) A Pattern 3 sentence is different from a Pattern 2 sentence because it has

a(n) _____.
       indirect object

7) In a noun-linking verb-adjective pattern, the adjective is called a

_____ adjective.
    predicate

Exercise C 9

Directions

Write what job each underlined word is doing in each sentence. Choose your answers from the following list:

subject *object of the preposition* *verb*
modifier *direct object* *indirect object*
predicate nominative *predicate adjective*

Sentence #	Word	Job
1	time	*object of the preposition*
1	tricks	*direct object*
2	treat	*predicate nominative*
3	sat	*verb*
3	funny	*modifier*
4	us	*indirect object*
4	eyes	*object of the preposition*
5	successful	*predicate adjective*

9 Playing with Words

Playing with Words

Some verbs can be action verbs in one sentence and linking verbs in another. These verbs include look, *taste, feel, smell, sound, remain, appear, stay,* and *grow*. We will use the verbs *grow* and *remain* both ways in the following examples:

grow

  Action verb: Plants grow seeds when they mature.

  Linking verb: Children grow restless when they have to sit for too long.

remain

  Action verb: The students remained in the classroom.

  Linking verb: Mrs. Wilson remained calm during the storm.

Now you try! You can change the subject and the verb form (*taste* becomes *tasted*, for example) if you want to.

taste

  Action verb

  _____

  _____

  Linking verb

  _____

  _____

feel

  Action verb

  _____

  _____

  Linking verb

  _____

  _____

smell

Action verb

_____

_____

Linking verb

_____

_____

look

Action verb

_____

_____

Linking verb

_____

_____

Look at the next page to see how you did!

9 PLAYING WITH WORDS

Playing with Words
How Did I Do?

If your answer is *yes*, each question below is worth one point.

Answer the following questions based on your student's work on the previous page. Then compare your answers with your student's.

1) Did you write a sentence in which *taste* is an action verb? _____

2) Did you write a sentence in which *taste* is a linking verb? _____

3) Did you write a sentence in which *feel* is an action verb? _____

4) Did you write a sentence in which *feel* is a linking verb? _____

5) Did you write a sentence in which *smell* is an action verb? _____

6) Did you write a sentence in which *smell* is a linking verb? _____

7) Did you write a sentence in which *look* is an action verb? _____

8) Did you write a sentence in which *look* is a linking verb? _____

9) Do you think you're a terrific kid? Give yourself two points! _____

Now, add up all of your points for your **total points!** _____

If you got 10 points, you did amazingly!

If you got 9 points, you did incredibly!

If you got 8 points, you did wonderfully!

If you got 7 points, you did a great job.

If you got 6 points, you made a good try.

Linking Verbs and Sentence Patterns 4 & 5: Assessment

Directions
The sentences below include all five of the sentence patterns. Parse all of the parts of speech and put parentheses around the prepositional phrases. Then diagram each sentence. Use The Process Chart! You can also look at the lesson notes if you need help.

              adv   *n*   *av*   *adj*   *adj*   *n*

$\underline{}$ **1)** <u>Sometimes</u>, collies need special grooming <u>treatments</u>.
 6

      pp *art* *adj*   *n*   *pp* *art*   *n*   *pn*   *lv* *art*   *n*

$\underline{}$ **2)** (After a long winter) (on the farm), Jenny was a <u>mess</u>!
 13

      adv *art* *adj*   *n*   *av* *pro* *art* *adj*   *n*

$\underline{}$ **3)** First, the dog <u>groomer</u> gave <u>her</u> a good bath.
 9

      art   *n*   *av*   *pp* *adj*   *pn*   *pp* *art* *adj*   *n*

$\underline{}$ **4)** The groomer <u>worked</u> (on poor Jenny) (for a long time).
 12

      pp *art*   *n*   *pp* *art*   *n*   *pn*   *lv*   *adj*

$\underline{}$ **5)** (By the end) (of the afternoon), Jenny was <u>gorgeous</u>!
 11

$\overline{\underline{}}$
 51

9 ASSESSMENT

Short answer
Each correct answer is worth one point.

___ 6) Write the three articles in English: _____ _____ _____

  3   a, an, the

___ 7) In a Pattern 4 (N-LV-N) sentence, the second noun is the _____.

  1   predicate nominative

___ 8) In a Pattern 5 (N-LV-ADJ) sentence, the adjective is the _____.

  1   predicate adjective

=====
  5

ASSESSMENT 9

Directions

Write what job the underlined words are doing in each sentence. Choose your answers from the following list:

subject *object of the preposition* *verb*
modifier *direct object* *indirect object*
predicate nominative *predicate adjective*

Each correct answer is worth one point.

Sentence #	Word	Job
1	Sometimes	*modifier*
1	treatments	*direct object*
2	mess	*predicate nominative*
3	groomer	*subject*
3	her	*indirect object*
4	worked	*verb*
5	gorgeous	*predicate adjective*

$\dfrac{}{7}$

Diagrams

Enter score from diagramming solutions here.

$\dfrac{}{35}$

$\dfrac{}{98}$ Total Points $\dfrac{78}{98} = 80\%$

Lesson 10
Helping Verbs

Instructor Notes

This unit requires some memorization, or, at least, it requires familiarity and the ability to quickly recognize a verb as a helping verb. The concept of "helping verb" is not difficult, but putting it into practice could be complicated if students can't recognize one when they see it. While they do not need to be able to rattle off all 23 helping verbs we introduce, they should be able to recall them from a prompt. We have built activities into each exercise to review the different groups of helping verbs. Encourage them to study the groups, write them a couple of times, say them aloud, or practice them in any other way that they may find helpful. Then, when they are working on each exercise, encourage them to look back at the list to complete the activity only **after** they've given it their very best try to recall the words.

The most important concept that your student needs to understand before attempting the exercises on their own is that, in a verb phrase, it's **only the last word** that is the **main verb**. The other verbs in the verb phrase, as long as they're on the list of helping verbs, are helping verbs. In fact, if there is a word in a "verb phrase" that isn't on the helping verb list and isn't a main verb...it's not a helping verb either. It's something else entirely (quite possibly an adverb!).

Adverbs, those sneaky little guys, like to hide inside verb phrases—either between a helping verb and the main verb, or, if there is more than one helping verb, between helping verbs. If your student finds a word in a verb phrase that is not a helping verb or a main verb, tell them to try to see if it's an adverb. They can do the movability test for adverbs (see Lesson 6) to check (because if it's cuddled up inside a verb phrase, it's almost certainly modifying the verb!).

It can be interesting to students to realize that we use helping verbs all the time to form questions in English. This is another example of English grammar that has been hardwired into your student's brain if they are a native speaker!

Diagramming solutions are found at the end of the book.

STUDENT NOTES

Lesson 10: Helping Verbs

We all could use a little help once in a while, couldn't we? Well, the same is true for verbs, if they want to be able to form certain *tenses*. A tense is a form of the verb that shows what **time** the verb is talking about.

Example: I **eat** strawberries. (*If anyone has strawberries, I am willing to eat them.*)

I **ate** strawberries. (*At some time in the past, there were strawberries and I ate them.*)

The only difference between the two sentences is the **verb tense**. In the first sentence, *eat* shows that the action is happening in the present, while *ate*, in the second sentence, shows that the action happened in the past.

What if we want to say that the strawberries are being eaten right this very second? You could say I **am eating** strawberries. (*Watch as I put the strawberries into my mouth, chew them up, and swallow them in real time!*)

We added another word to the verb to form this tense: *am*. This little word is called a **helping verb**.

When you add a helping verb to a verb, you form a **verb phrase**. A verb phrase is a group of words that work together to do the job of one verb.

> A **phrase** is a group of words that work together to do a job in a sentence. You already know one kind: a **prepositional phrase**. A prepositional phrase is a group of words that work together as a modifier. A verb phrase is a group of words that work together as a verb.

A verb phrase may have two, three, or even four words in it. The last verb in the verb phrase is the **main verb**. The rest of the words are **helping verbs**. The helping verbs tell you when the main verb happens. Look at these examples:

I **will hit** a homerun.   verb phrase: **will hit**
                                              helping verb: **will**
                                              main verb: **hit**

I **have been reading** a book.   verb phrase: **have been reading**
                                              helping verbs: **have been**
                                              main verb: **reading**

I **should have been listening**!   verb phrase: **should have been listening**
                                              helping verbs: **should have been**
                                              main verb: **listening**

The **main verb** is the one that will be either an **action verb** or a **linking verb**. You should still use The Process Chart to figure out which kind of verb you have, but use the entire verb phrase when you are asking, "(subject) (verb) what?" For instance, look at one of our example sentences above: **I have been reading a book**. The subject is **I** and the verb (use the entire verb phrase!) is **have been reading**. That means our question is, "*I have been reading* what?" The answer to that question is **book**. So therefore, we have a Pattern 3 N-V-N sentence:
N (I) - V (have been reading) - N (book).

This list includes the most common helping verbs:

"be" linking verbs (sometimes helping verbs)	sometimes helping verbs	modal verbs (always helping verbs)	
is	has	will	may
am	have	would	might
are	had	shall	must
was	do	should	
were	does	can	
be	did	could	
being			
been			

> **Modals**
> **Modals** are always helping verbs. You will never see a modal by itself, unless the main verb is implied:
>
> "Are you going to the party?" "I might [*go to the party*]."
>
> The part in the brackets is implied, so the modal *might* is still working with a main verb, even though it's not said out loud.
>
> Another interesting thing about modals is that they never change, regardless of the subject! For example, *I shall, you shall, he/she/it shall* (never **shalls**).

Did you notice that some of these helping verbs can also be linking verbs (look at the first column, *"be" linking verbs*)? It's easy to tell if "be" verbs are linking verbs or helping verbs, though. If you have a verb phrase, only the **last verb** (the **main verb**) in the phrase is going to be either an action verb or a linking verb. As long as the other words in the verb phrase are on the helping verb list, they're helping verbs and are marked with **hv**.

                  pn   hv   lv art adj   n

Example: John will be a fourth grader.

Will be is the verb phrase, and *be* is a linking verb. *Be* is also the main verb because it is the last verb in the verb phrase. The entire verb phrase is acting as a linking verb, because *John* and *grader* are the same person.

                  pn   hv hv av pp adj   n

Example: John will be going (to fourth grade).

Will be going is the verb phrase, and *going* is an action verb. *Be* is a helping verb in this sentence because it's not the last word in the verb phrase. So when you're using The Process Chart, be sure you're using the **entire verb phrase** when you ask your questions, but remember that the verb that you need to identify as an action verb or linking verb is the **last** verb.

The second column, called *sometimes helping verbs*, includes verbs that may or may not be helping verbs.

Example: I **do** origami. (action verb)
I **do** want to come with you! (helping verb)

John **has** a guitar. (action verb)
John **has** practiced a lot. (helping verb)

Diagramming helping verbs:

This is an easy one! Just put all of the verbs in the verb place! Here's the diagram of the first sentence above:

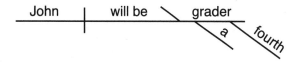

If you want to take the sentence above and make it a question, take the first helping verb and move it in front of the subject:

Will John **be** a fourth grader?

If a sentence has a helping verb in it, that's how you make it into a question. Can you see the difference in the diagram?

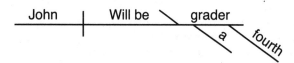

That's right: **Will** has a capital letter. That's because it's the first word of the question!

Guess what? If you are a native English speaker, you already use helping verbs all the time! What if a sentence only has one verb (the main verb) and we want to make it into a question? How would you make a question out of the following sentence?

Mr. Janes **made** an apple pie.

You would say:

Did Mr. Janes **make** an apple pie?

You have to add a helping verb to make it into a question!

> Be on the lookout! Adverbs just *love* to sneak between a helping verb and the main verb, like this: *I could totally eat a horse!* Think of a big pile of golden retrievers taking a nap, and a little kitten climbs into the middle and makes itself comfy. If a word isn't on your helping verb list, it's **not** a helping verb. So if it's not a main verb, either, it's probably a sneaky little adverb modifying the verb! Luckily, you know the adverb movability test to find out.

EXERCISE A **10**

Helping Verbs: Exercise A

Directions

Parse (mark) all of the parts of speech in the sentences below and put the prepositional phrases in parentheses. Remember, helping verbs are marked with **hv**. Then diagram the sentences. Use The Process Chart and the lesson notes to help you.

    adv   adj   n   hv   av pp art   n

1) Today, our class will go (to the library).

    pro hv   hv   av   art adj   n   adv*

2) I will be checking a new book out.

If necessary, remind your student that, to be a preposition, a word needs to be in a prepositional phrase. Prepositions by themselves, like out *in this sentence, are usually adverbs.*

    pro hv   lv   adj   n

3) We are becoming good readers.

    hv pro   av   art adj   n

4) Do you want a new book?

(Remember how to diagram a question? Look back through your lesson notes if you need help!)

    hv adv   av   adj   adj   n

5) Do not lose your library book!

(Remember how to diagram a command? Look back through your lesson notes if you need help!)

10 Exercise A

Directions
Write what job the underlined words are doing in each sentence. Choose your answers from the following list:

subject   *object of the preposition*   *verb*
modifier   *direct object*   *indirect object*
predicate nominative   *predicate adjective*

Sentence #	Word	Job
1	Today	*modifier*
2	will be checking	*verb*
3	readers	*predicate nominative*
4	you	*subject*
5	book	*direct object*

Directions
In the notes for this lesson, there is a list of all of the helping verbs. Look at the eight verbs in the first column—the one called **"be" linking verbs**. Study them closely, say them out loud, and write them down a couple of times. Then, without looking, see how many of them you can write from memory! If you don't get all eight from memory, be sure to look back for the ones you missed and write them in the remaining blanks:

is	*were*
am	*be*
are	*being*
was	*been*

Students usually memorize these words in order; however, it doesn't matter what order the words are written in.

Helping Verbs: Exercise B

Directions
Parse all of the parts of speech in the sentences below and put the prepositional phrases in parentheses. Remember, helping verbs are marked with **hv**. Then diagram the sentences. Use The Process Chart and the lesson notes to help you.

    art   n   hv   lv   pro pp adj   adj   n

1) The library has become one (of my <u>favorite</u> places).

    pro pp art   n   pp art   n   hv hv av pp   n

2) All (of the knowledge) (of the world) <u>can be found</u> (in books).

    hv   pro   av   pro

3) Can <u>you</u> imagine that?

    pro hv   adv   av   art   n

4) I have <u>always</u> loved the library.

    pro hv av adv pp art adj   n   adv

5) I can curl up (with a good <u>book</u>) anytime!

Directions
Write what job the underlined words are doing in each sentence. Choose your answers from the following list:

    subject   *object of the preposition*   *verb*
    modifier   *direct object*   *indirect object*
    predicate nominative   *predicate adjective*

Sentence #	Word	Job
1	favorite	*modifier*
2	can be found	*verb*
3	you	*subject*
4	always	*modifier*
5	book	*object of the preposition*

10 EXERCISE B

Directions

Study the list of *sometimes* helping verbs in column 2 of the chart in the lesson notes. Write them a couple of times until you think that you know them all. Copy those six verbs onto the lines provided, then use them to fill in the crossword puzzle. One letter has been given to you; use that letter to figure out how the words all fit.

Hint: Count the number of letters. There is one word that can only go in one space!

Crossword Puzzle

_____has_____

_____have_____

_____had_____

_____do_____

_____does_____

_____did_____

Helping Verbs: Exercise C

Directions
Parse all of the parts of speech in the sentences below and put the prepositional phrases in parentheses. Then diagram the sentences. Use The Process Chart and the lesson notes to help you.

    adj   adj   n   hv   av   pp —— pn ——
1) My favorite book was written (by P.L. Travers).

    art   n   hv   lv —— pn ——
2) The book is called *Mary Poppins*.

    art   adj   adj   n   hv   av   adj   n   adv
3) The naughty Banks children have driven their nanny away.

—— pn ——   hv   av   art   adj   n   pp   art   adj   adj   n
4) Mary Poppins has answered the newspaper ad (for the Bankses' new nanny).

    art   adj   n   hv   av   pp   adj   adj   n   pp —— pn ——
5) The Banks children are taken (on many magical adventures) (by Mary Poppins).

Directions
Write what job the underlined words are doing in each sentence. Choose your answers from the following list:

    subject   *object of the preposition*   *verb*
    modifier   *direct object*   *indirect object*
    predicate nominative   *predicate adjective*

Sentence #	Word	Job
1	favorite	*modifier*
2	book	*subject*
3	away	*modifier*
4	ad	*direct object*
5	adventures	*object of the preposition*

10 Exercise C

Directions
Study the column called *modal verbs* in the helping verbs chart in the lesson notes. Without looking at the list, find and circle all of the modals that you can, and write them on the blanks below the word search. Words may be across, down, and diagonal. If you can't find all of them, look back to see which ones you are missing, find them, and write them on the list. Good luck!

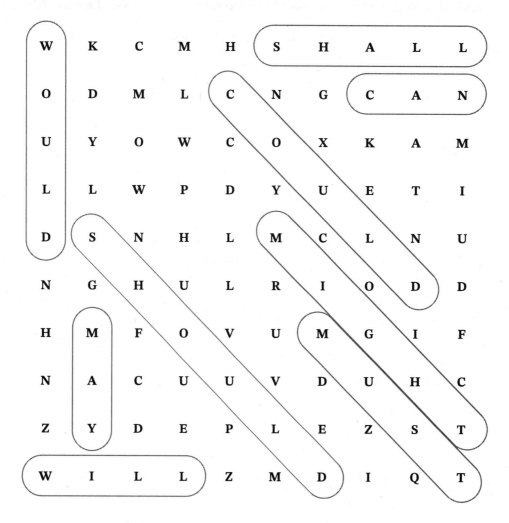

will	*should*
would	*may*
can	*might*
could	*must*
shall	

Playing with Words

You learned about a group of helping verbs called *modals*. You know that these verbs are always helping verbs. Now let's talk a little more about what modals do. Look at these three sentences:

I **would** go to the party.   I **could** go to the party.   I **should** go to the party.

Do they all say the same thing? Almost—but not quite. Let's add a little more to each sentence to make it clearer:

I **would** go to the party, *but I've got to help my mom at home first.*
I *would* go means that I intend to go if I can—for example, if I can get my work done at home, I will go.

I **could** go to the party *if it were on a weekend.*
I *could go* means that it may be possible for me to go under certain circumstances.

I **should** go to the party *because they are expecting me.*
I *should go* means I'm supposed to go.

See how they are all a little bit different? Modals are used to create the *conditional* mood. Look back up at our expanded examples: the parts that we added to make them clearer are all *conditions* that need to be met. When we say "I go," there are no conditions: I'm going right now and that's that. We add modals when we want to express something more complicated.

Now it's your turn! Below are three more little sentences, using the same modal helping verbs. Can you add conditions to the sentences that show the differences among the three? Look back at what each modal means. Make your conditions as silly and funny as you can dream up! And remember, it's okay to ask for help!

I **would** write to my aunt, but

_____

_____

I **could** write to my aunt, if

_____

_____

I **should** write to my aunt, because

_____

_____

Now let's try it with a couple of other helping verbs that aren't modals:

I *was writing* to my aunt when

_____

_____

I *should have* written to my aunt, but

_____

_____

Now, turn to the next page and total up your points!

Playing with Words
How Did I Do?

If you completed these sentences and they make sense, give yourself two points each:

Answer the following questions based on your student's work on the previous page. Then compare your answers with your student's.

1) I would write to my aunt, but — _____

2) I could write to my aunt, if — _____

3) I should write to my aunt, because — _____

4) I was writing to my aunt when — _____

5) I should have written to my aunt, but — _____

Now, add up all of your points for your **total points!** _____

If you got 10 points, you did amazingly!

If you got 9 points, you did incredibly!

If you got 8 points, you did wonderfully!

If you got 7 points, you did a great job.

If you got 6 points, you made a good try.

10 Assessment

Helping Verbs: Assessment

Directions

Parse all of the parts of speech in the sentences below and put the prepositional phrases in parentheses. Then diagram the sentences. Use The Process Chart and the lesson notes to help you.

         pn   hv   av   adj   n   art adv   adj   n

__9__ 1) Billy was asking his family a very important question.

       hv   pro   av   adj   adj   n

__6__ 2) "Has anyone seen my library book?"

      pro   hv   lv   adv   adj

__5__ 3) He was feeling rather panicky.

      pro   hv   av   adv

__4__ 4) It was due tomorrow!

      art   n   hv   av   pp art   n   pp adj   n

__12__ 5) The book was lying (on the floor) (under his bed).

__36__

ASSESSMENT 10

Directions

Write what job the underlined words are doing in each sentence. Choose your answers from the following list:

subject   *object of the preposition*   *verb*
modifier   *direct object*   *indirect object*
predicate nominative   *predicate adjective*

Each correct answer is worth one point.

Sentence #	Word	Job
1	family	indirect object
2	anyone	subject
2	book	direct object
3	panicky	predicate adjective
4	tomorrow	modifier
5	was lying	verb
5	bed	object of preposition

7

10 ASSESSMENT

Helping verbs
Write as many of the helping verbs as you can from memory. Each one is worth one point. The first letter of each word has been given to you.

i*s*	h*as*	w*ill*	m*ay*
a*m*	h*ave*	w*ould*	m*ight*
a*re*	h*ad*	s*hall*	m*ust*
w*as*	d*o*	s*hould*	
w*ere*	d*oes*	c*an*	
b*e*	d*id*	c*ould*	
b*eing*			
b*een*			

___
23

Diagrams
Enter score from diagramming solutions here.

___
28

___ Total Points $\dfrac{75}{94} = 80\%$
94

Lesson 11
Conjunctions & Compounds

Instructor Notes

This is the last lesson in the book! Your student has learned so many things about grammar. They've learned that they already know a lot about grammar, and now they have words to label and organize what they know. This final lesson is kind of a slam dunk, because there are little hints (in the form of where to look for compound situations of the type being used) in the exercises and the assessment.

Diagramming solutions are found at the end of the book.

Lesson 11: Conjunctions & Compounds

Can you believe that this is the last lesson in this book? You have learned so much already! Well, you already knew a lot of grammar—you just might not have known how to label things and how to make sense of the organization of words. But now, you are ready to learn the second-to-last of the nine parts of speech!

You have already learned about:

> nouns
> articles
> adjectives
> pronouns
> prepositions (and prepositional phrases)
> verbs
> adverbs

Now, you just need to add **conjunctions**, and you will be able to parse and make sense of just about any sentence you come across!

Conjunctions
Conjunctions are used to join things together in a sentence. One of the few rules you need to know is that they can **only join things that are the same part of speech**.

So, you can join nouns: The **cat** and the **dog** walked down the road. (*You can also join a noun and a pronoun, since they both name a person, place, thing, or idea.*)
You can join verbs: The children **walked** and **ran** to school.
You can join adverbs: The cat moved **slowly, quietly,** and **carefully.**
You can join prepositional phrases: **Over the river and through the woods**, to Grandmother's house we go.
You can even join sentences: **I walked to the corner** and **the cat came to meet me.**

Or anything else, as long as the two (or more!) things being joined are alike!

But...

> **You can't join things that aren't alike.**
> The children **walked** and **table**. Huh?

By now, you've probably realized that *and* is a conjunction. It's not the only one, though. There are six more main conjunctions that you can use to make a *compound situation*.

The seven main conjunctions you need to know about now are:

<u>f</u>or (*when it means **because***)	<u>b</u>ut
<u>a</u>nd	<u>o</u>r
<u>n</u>or	<u>y</u>et (*when it means **but***)
	<u>s</u>o

> Here's an easy way to remember these conjunctions: What do you notice about the first letter of each word if you read down each column? That's right! They spell out ***FANBOYS***. It's a silly, fun way to remember the seven main conjunctions!

The most common conjunctions are **and, but, so,** and **or. Nor** is a fancier, negative conjunction for when you're saying things like, "Neither rain **nor** sleet **nor** dead of night will stop us!" It means none of those three things will stop us—but it sounds a little more dramatic and exciting. **For** isn't one we use often today, but if you read older books, you might see things like, "I cannot marry you, **for** I love another!" You will hear **yet** in sentences like, "I have chores to do, **yet** I don't want to move." If you can substitute **but** for **yet**, you know that **yet** is doing its conjunction job. Go ahead and try it in that sentence: I have chores to do, **but** I don't want to move.

> **Compounds**
> The two (or more) alike things that are joined by a conjunction create a **compound**. A **compound** is one thing that is made up of two or more alike things. So, if you join two nouns and use them as a subject (*Mika and Janie are friends*), you make a compound subject. If you join two sentences, you make a compound sentence. If you join two prepositional phrases...well, you probably get the idea. Calling it a **"compound"** is just a fancy way to say that you've joined two or more alike things together with a conjunction. Parse (mark) conjunctions as **conj**.

When you have to diagram a sentence that includes a compound of any kind, first look at the compound like it is only one thing. Where would that one thing go in the diagram? A compound subject would be the first thing on the baseline, for example. A compound prepositional phrase would be attached to whatever it is modifying. To make room for the compound thing, though, you need to make a branch on whatever line it goes on. Don't worry! Here's exactly what those branches look like for all kinds of compound things.

A) Compound subject

```
 pn   conj  pn    av     adv
John  and  Jim  walked  home.
```

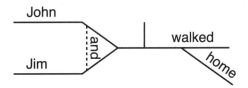

B) Compound verb

```
  pp   adj    n   pro  av   conj   av
(On  most  days,)  I  stretch  and  exercise.
```

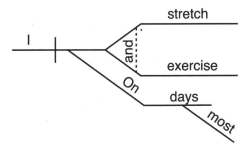

In this sentence, we have a prepositional phrase (*On most days*) that is modifying both parts of the compound verb. Notice that it is attached **before** the baseline is branched apart, because it modifies **both** of the verbs.

11 STUDENT NOTES

  pn *av* *conj* *av* *art* *adj* *n*
Norio raked and mowed the front yard.

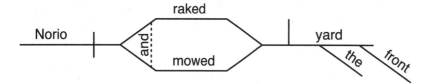

Notice that the two verbs in the sentence above share a direct object. That's why we joined them back together again after the verbs, before we added the direct object to the baseline.

  pn *av* *adj* *n* *conj* *av* *adj* *n*
Norio cleaned his room and did his chores.

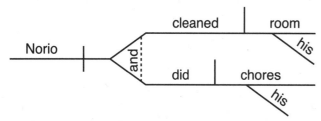

In this sentence, each verb has its own direct object, so we don't need to join the baseline back together.

C) Compound direct object

  pn *av* *art* *n* *conj* *n*
Susana ate a sandwich and chips.

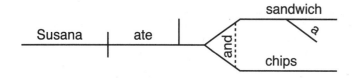

D) Compound indirect object

  pn *av* *pn* *conj* *pro* *n*
Susana sent Norio and me presents.

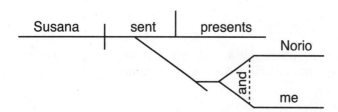

E) **Compound predicate nominative or predicate adjective**

pro lv adj conj adj
She felt hungry and tired.

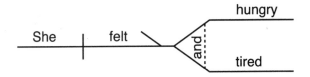

F) **Compound prepositional phrases**

pro av pp art n conj pp art n
We ran (down the stairs) and (out the door).

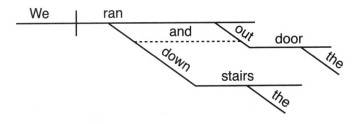

G) **Prepositional phrase with compound object of the preposition**

pro av pp art adj n conj n
She dusted (under the new table and chairs).

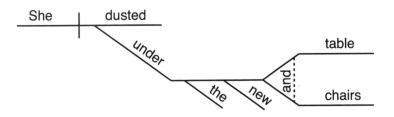

Can you tell why *the* and *new* aren't attached to either *table* or *chairs*? Why would these words be attached to the line before it branches off?

*These words modify **both** table and chairs.*

11 STUDENT NOTES

H) Compound sentence

    pn   *av*   *art*   *n*   *conj*   *pn*   *av* *pro*
Jason mowed the lawn and Susana raked it.

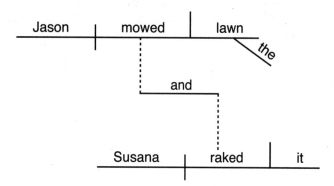

Connect compound sentences at the verbs.

I) Compound modifiers

  art *adj* *conj* *adj*   *n*   *av*
The black and white dog barked.

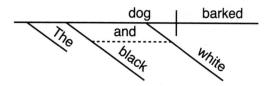

J) Three or more of something

 pn *pn* *conj* *pn* *av*   *n*
Ed, Joe, and Jim ate lunch.

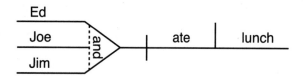

Wait...we told you there are NINE parts of speech!
Great catch; we sure did! The last part of speech is an **interjection! Interjections** show emotion or excitement: words like "Hey," or "Wow!" or "Awesome!" are all interjections. They don't even need to be words. "Ouch," "ah," "ooh," and "hmmm" are all interjections, too. They aren't always just one word: "Fancy that!" and other expressions of surprise are also interjections. These are set apart from the rest of the sentence with either an exclamation point (!) or a comma (,) depending on how strong the emotion is. Sometimes, they have a question mark, like "Huh?" or "Hmm?" If you're parsing the sentence, mark an interjection with *int* (use wings if it's more than one word). And the best news is, because it's not grammatically a part of the sentence, you just diagram an interjection on its own little floating line, like this:

Holy cow! The Cubs won the World Series!

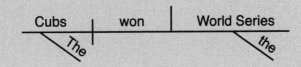

You can diagram it this way even if it's set apart with a comma.

11 EXERCISE A

Conjunctions & Compounds: Exercise A

Directions
Parse (mark) all of the parts of speech in the sentences below and put parentheses around all of the prepositional phrases. Diagram each sentence. Be sure to look at the hints given with each sentence that tell you where to look in the notes for help with your diagrams.

1) (See Notes A)

    adj   n   conj   n   hv   av   pro
    My aunt and uncle are visiting us.

2) (See Notes B)

    pro   av   n   conj   av   n
    They bring presents and take pictures.

3) (See Notes C)

    int pro av adj n conj n
    Boy, I love my aunt and uncle.

4) (See Notes D)

    pro adv av adj n conj pro n
    They always take my sister and me places.

5) (See Notes E)

    adj   n   lv   adv   adj conj adj
    My relatives are always energetic and fun.

Fill in the blank

6) If using a conjunction to join things, the things must be

    _____.

    the same part of speech

7) Adverbs modify _____, _____,

    and _____.

    verbs, adjectives, other adverbs

Exercise A 11

Directions
Write what job each underlined word is doing in each sentence. Choose your answers from the following list:

subject *object of the preposition* *verb*
modifier *direct object* *indirect object*
predicate nominative *predicate adjective*

Sentence #	Word	Job
1	are visiting	*verb*
2	They	*subject*
3	aunt	*direct object*
4	always	*modifier*
5	energetic	*predicate adjective*

11 EXERCISE B

Conjunctions & Compounds: Exercise B

Directions
Parse all of the parts of speech in the sentences below and put the prepositional phrases in parentheses. Diagram each sentence. The clues above each sentence tell you where to look in the notes for help with your diagrams.

1) (See Notes F)

    adj   n   av   pp art   n   conj pp art   n
    My grandparents travel (in a motorhome) or (on a <u>plane</u>).

2) (See Notes G)

    pn   av   art   n   pp art   n   conj art   adj   n
    Grandpa drives the motorhome (down the highways and the <u>country</u> roads).

3) (See Notes H)

    pn   av pro pp art   n   conj   pn   adv   av   pp pro
    Grandpa does most (of the driving), but Grandma sometimes helps (with <u>it</u>).

4) (See Notes I)

    adj adj conj adj   n   lv adj   adj   n
    Their tan and white motorhome is their favorite <u>place</u>.

5) (See Notes J)

    adv   pn   pn   conj pro av   pp art   n
    Yesterday, Grandma, Grandpa, and I <u>went</u> (to the lake).

6) **Circle the part of speech below that is NOT a modifier**

    prepositional phrase   *article*   *adjective*   (*helping verb*)   *adverb*

Fill in the blank

7) In a noun-linking verb-adjective pattern (Pattern 5), the adjective is called the

    _____.

    predicate adjective

Exercise B 11

Directions

Write what job the underlined words are doing in each sentence. Choose your answers from the following list:

subject *object of the preposition* *verb*
modifier *direct object* *indirect object*
predicate nominative *predicate adjective*

Sentence #	Word	Job
1	plane	*object of the preposition*
2	country	*modifier*
3	it	*object of the preposition*
4	place	*predicate nominative*
5	went	*verb*

11 EXERCISE C

Conjunctions & Compounds: Exercise C

Directions
Parse all of the parts of speech and put parentheses around the prepositional phrases. Diagram all of the sentences. Watch for the little clues given above each sentence!

1) (See Notes G)

    adj   n   av   pp   pn   conj   pn
    My family consists (of Americans and Canadians).

2) (See Notes H)

    adv adj   n   av pp   pn   conj adv adj   n   av   pp   pn
    My dad's parents live (in Quebec), but my mom's family comes (from Virginia).

3) (See Notes J)

    adv adj   n   n   conj   n   lv   adv adj pp adj   n
    My mom's parents, brothers, and sisters are very close (to each other).

4) (See Notes A)

    adv adj   n   conj   n   av adj   adj   n
    My dad's mom and dad have no other children.

5) (See Notes C)

    int pro av   adj   n   conj adj   n
    Yes, we love Dad's parents and Mom's parents.

Fill in the blank

6) The items on the baseline of an N-LV-N sentence are the _____,
the _____, and the _____.
    subject, verb, predicate nominative

7) A pronoun can do any job that a _____ can do.
    noun

Exercise C 11

Directions

Write what job the underlined words are doing in each sentence. Choose your answers from the following list:

subject *object of the preposition* *verb*
modifier *direct object* *indirect object*
predicate nominative *predicate adjective*

Sentence #	Word	Job
1	Americans	object of the preposition
2	dad's	modifier
3	close	predicate adjective
4	mom	subject
5	parents	direct object

11 Playing with Words

Playing with Words

For this activity, think of any two nouns you want. You can choose from the Noun Bank below, or you can make up your own. Then write a sentence using them together in a compound as the part of speech shown. There is an example of each kind of compound so you can see what to do. As always, look back at the notes if you need help!

Noun Bank

kangaroo	*zebra*	*iguana*	*sunflower*
cheeseburger	*sandwich*	*book*	*pencil*
car	*airplane*	*street*	*sidewalk*
house	*shed*	*sand*	*ribbon*
ball	*paper*	*scissors*	*gravel*

For all of the examples, we're going to use *puppy* and *kitten* as our two nouns. For your own sentences, you can choose the same two nouns for each, or you can choose different nouns for each one. Have fun!

Compound subject

Example: The *puppy* and the *kitten* were asleep in their basket.

Your nouns: _____kangaroo_____ and _____zebra_____

Your sentence: ___The kangaroo and the zebra bounced along the forest path together___.

1) **Compound direct object**

   Example: I saw the *puppy* and the *kitten* through the window.

   Your nouns: _____ and _____

   Your sentence:

   _____

   _____

2) **Compound indirect object**

   Example: I gave the *puppy* and the *kitten* something to eat.

   Your nouns: _____ and _____

   Your sentence:

   _____

   _____

3) Compound object of the preposition

Example: I looked for the *puppy* and the *kitten*.

Your nouns: _____ and _____

Your sentence:

_____

_____

4) Compound predicate nominative

Example: The winners of the pet show were the *puppy* and the *kitten*.

Your nouns: _____ and _____

Your sentence:

_____

_____

Finally, think of two adjectives (or choose from the Adjective Bank) and write a sentence that uses them together as a compound predicate adjective.

Adjective Bank

big	*small*	*tiny*	*angry*
sad	*blue*	*red*	*pleased*
fluffy	*soft*	*scratchy*	*hard*

For our example, the adjectives are *happy* and *carefree*.

5) Compound predicate adjective

Example: I was *happy* and *carefree* on my vacation.

Your adjectives: _____ and _____

Your sentence:

_____

_____

Now, turn the page to see how you did on this activity!

Playing with Words
How Did I Do?

For each question that you can answer with *"yes,"* give yourself one point:

Answer the following questions based on your student's work on the previous page. Then compare your answers with your student's.

1) Did you use both of your nouns in your sentence? _____

    Did you use the nouns as a compound direct object? _____

2) Did you use both of your nouns in your sentence? _____

    Did you use the nouns as a compound indirect object? _____

3) Did you use both of your nouns in your sentence? _____

    Did you use the nouns as a compound object of the preposition? _____

4) Did you use both of your nouns in your sentence? _____

    Did you use the nouns as a compound predicate nominative? _____

5) Did you use both of your adjectives in your sentence? _____

    Did you use the adjectives as a compound predicate adjective? _____

Now, add up all of your points for your **total points:** _____

If you got 10 points, you did amazingly!

If you got 9 points, you did incredibly!

If you got 8 points, you did wonderfully!

If you got 7 points, you did a great job.

If you got 6 points, you made a good try.

Conjunctions & Compounds: Assessment

Directions
Parse all of the parts of speech and put parentheses around the prepositional phrases. Diagram all of the sentences. Remember to use The Process and the lesson notes if you need help. Watch for the little clues given before each sentence!

$\frac{}{10}$ **1)** (See Notes A)

      n   conj   n   lv adv   adj   pp adj   n

Friends and relatives are very <u>important</u> (to my <u>family</u>).

$\frac{}{15}$ **2)** (See Notes F)

  pro pp pro   av pp adj   n   conj pp art adj   n

<u>Most</u> (of them) live (in our town) or (in the next county).

$\frac{}{11}$ **3)** (See Notes C)

   int   adv   pro hv   av   art adj   n   conj adj   n

Hooray! Tomorrow, we will have a <u>huge</u> barbecue and family <u>reunion</u>.

$\frac{}{14}$ **4)** (See Notes H)

  art   n   hv   av   n   conj art   n   hv   av   pp adj   pro

The kids <u>will play</u> games and the <u>grownups</u> will visit (with each other).

$\frac{}{14}$ **5)** (See Notes D)

  art   n   hv   av   adj   n   conj   n   art   n   pp adj   n

The party will give our <u>relatives</u> and friends a chance (for <u>new</u> friendships).

$\frac{\overline{}}{64}$

11 ASSESSMENT

Short answer

Each correct answer is worth one point.

____ 6) Pronouns are words that _____.

1   take the place of nouns

____ 7) Adjectives are words that _____.

1   modify nouns and pronouns

____ 8) A sentence needs to have a subject and a _____.

1   verb

═══
 3

Assessment 11

Directions

Write what job the underlined words are doing in each sentence. Choose your answers from the following list:

subject   object of the preposition   verb
modifier   direct object   indirect object
predicate nominative   predicate adjective

Each correct answer is worth one point.

Sentence #	Word	Job
1	important	*predicate adjective*
1	family	*object of the preposition*
2	Most	*subject*
3	huge	*modifier*
3	reunion	*direct object*
4	will play	*verb*
4	grownups	*subject*
5	relatives	*indirect object*
5	new	*modifier*

9

Diagrams

Enter score from diagramming solutions here.

45

Total Points $\dfrac{97}{121} = 80\%$

121

Lesson 4: Prepositions

Exercise A

1)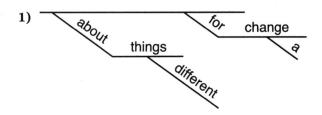

2)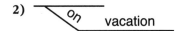

3)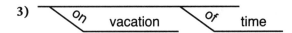

4)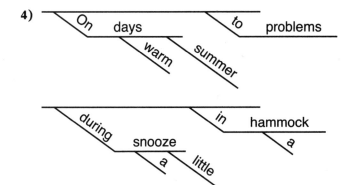

4 DIAGRAMS: EXERCISE B

Exercise B

1)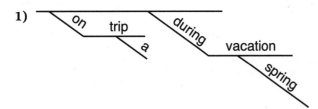

2)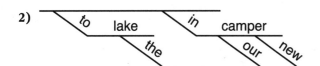

3)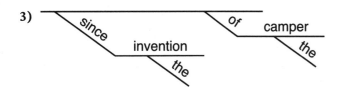

4)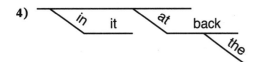

5)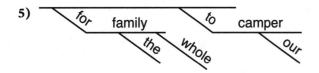

Exercise C

1)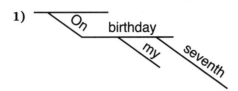

2)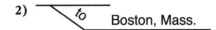

3)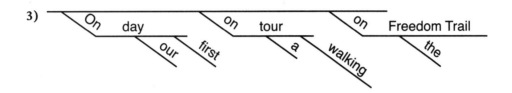

4)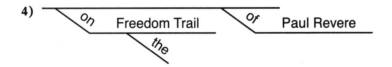

5)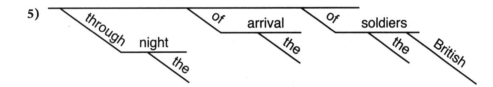

4 Diagrams: Assessment

Assessment

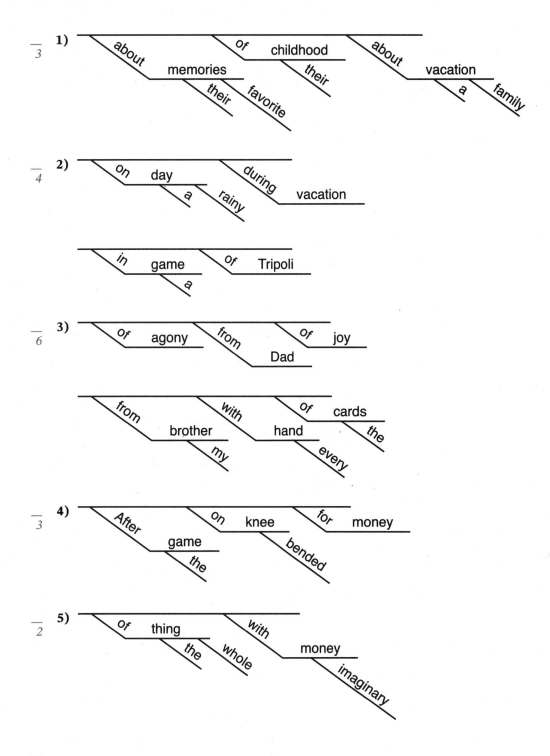

Diagrams

Enter score from diagramming solutions here.

___ *Total Points*
18

Lesson 5: Subject and Verb

Exercise A

1)
```
  mom   |  gave
 \      |
  \His
```

2)
```
 (you)  |  Clean
```

3)
```
  He    |  put
```

4)
```
  he    |  made
```

5)
```
  She   |  praised
```

5 DIAGRAMS: EXERCISE B

Exercise B

1)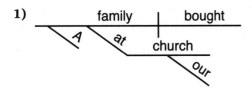

2)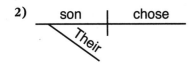

3)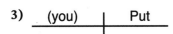

4)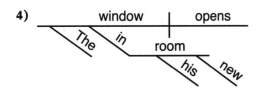

5)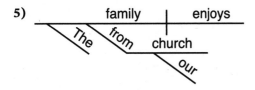

Exercise C

1)

2)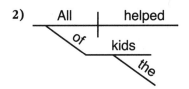

3)
```
   they   |   rushed
_____|_____
```

4)
```
   (you)  |  Imagine
_____|_____
```

5)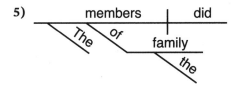

5 Diagrams: Assessment

Assessment

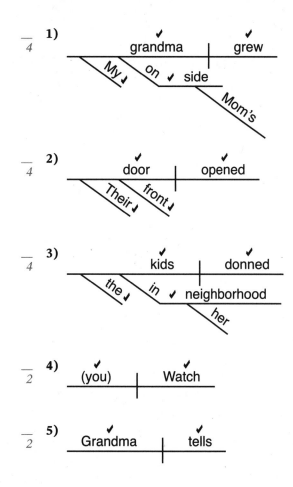

Diagrams

Enter score from diagramming solutions here.

═ Total Points
16

Lesson 6: Adverbs
Exercise A

1)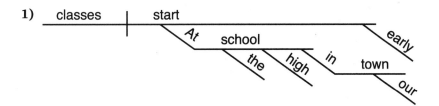

2)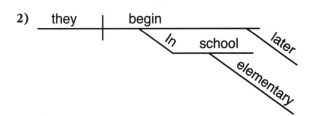

3)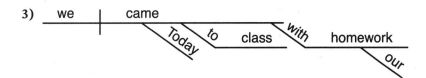

4)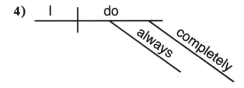

5)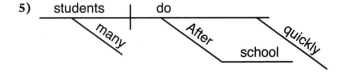

Exercise B

1)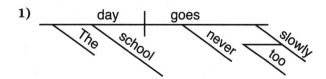

2)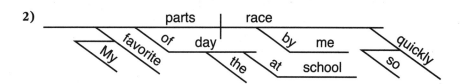

3)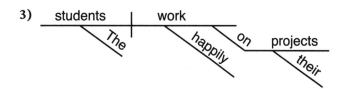

4)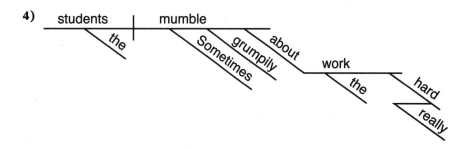

5)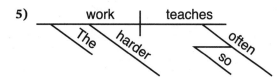

Exercise C

1)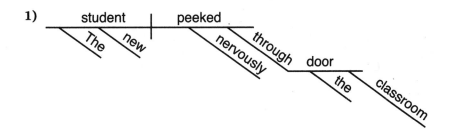

2)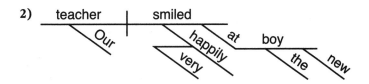

3)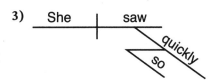

4)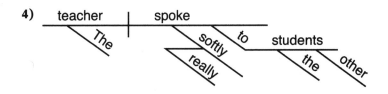

5)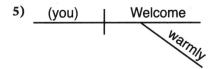

6 Diagrams: Assessment

Assessment

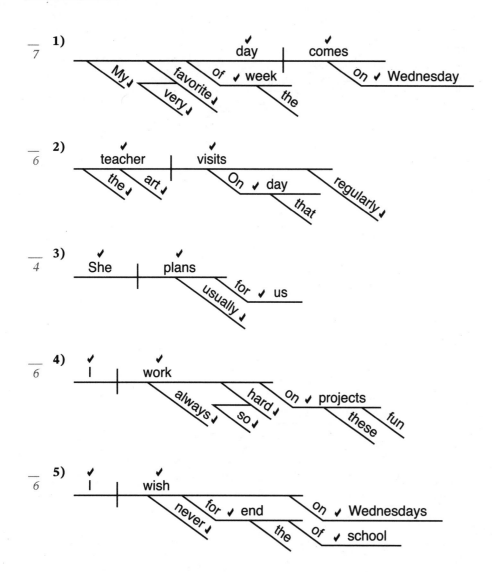

Diagrams

Enter score from diagramming solutions here.

= *Total Points*
29

Lesson 7: Sentence Patterns 1 and 2

Exercise A

1)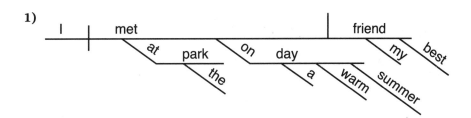

2)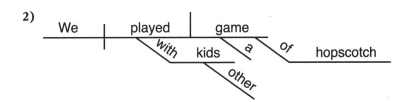

3)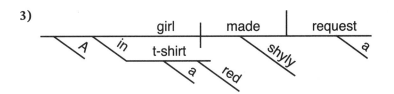

4)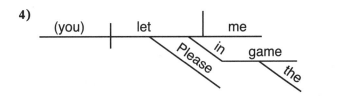

5)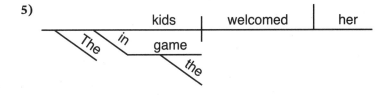

7 Diagrams: Exercise B

Exercise B

1)
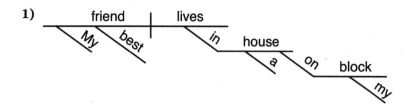

Your student may have on my block *modifying* lives; *this is not incorrect, as the sentence* My best friend lives on my block *is perfectly fine. Instead, take the opportunity to point out that it could also be modifying* house *in this case.*

2)
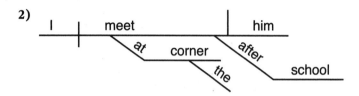

3)
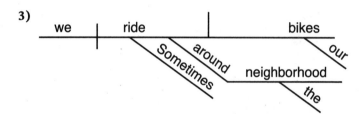

4)
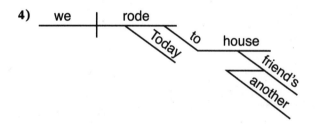

5)
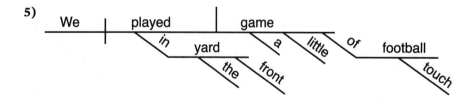

Exercise C

1)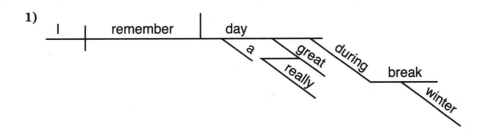

2)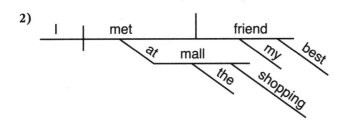

3)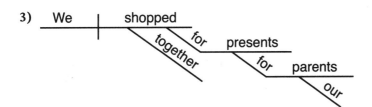

4)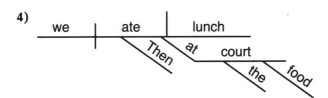

5)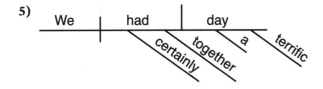

7 Diagrams: Assessment

Assessment

The vertical line between the verb and direct object is worth one point. Remember that properly diagrammed prepositional phrases are worth a total of one point.

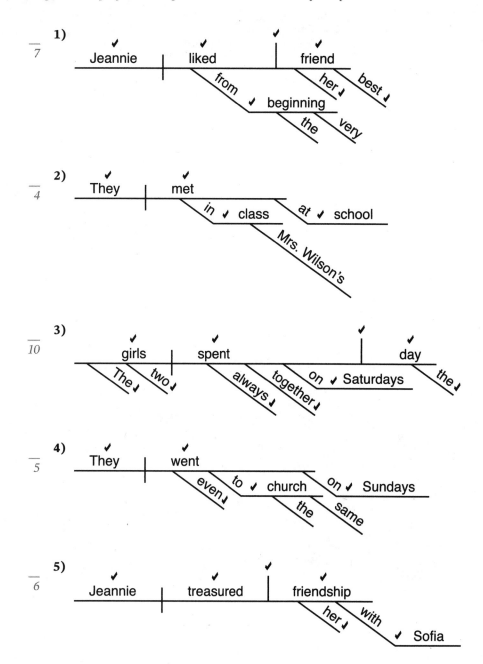

Diagrams

Enter score from diagramming solutions here.

===== *Total Points*
32

Lesson 8: Sentence Pattern 3
Exercise A

1)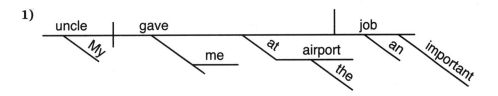

2)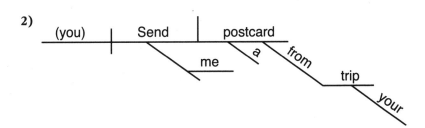

3)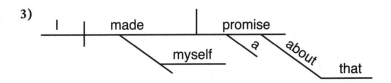

4)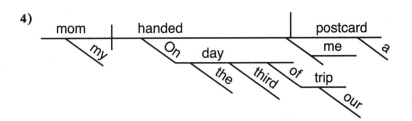

5)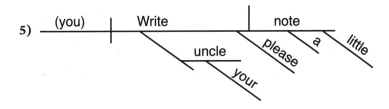

Exercise B

1)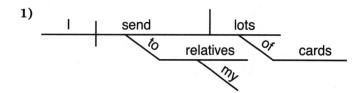

2)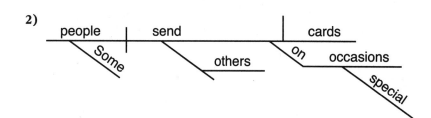

3)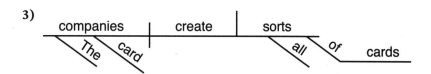

4)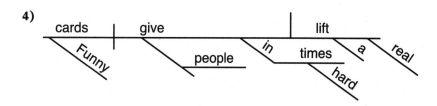

5)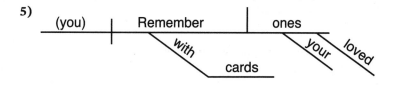

Exercise C

1)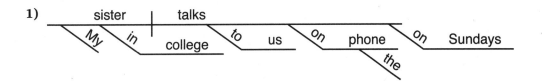

2)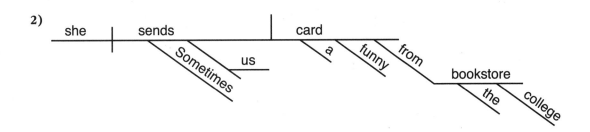

3)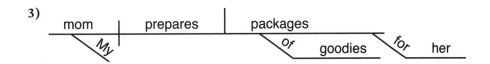

4)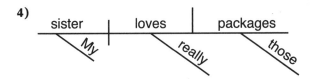

5)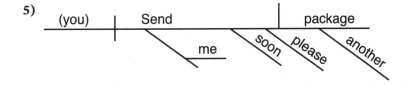

8 Diagrams: Assessment

Assessment

1) $\overline{}$ 5
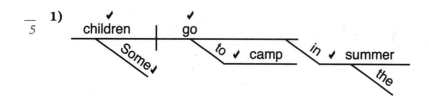

2) $\overline{}$ 7
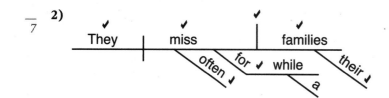

3) $\overline{}$ 12
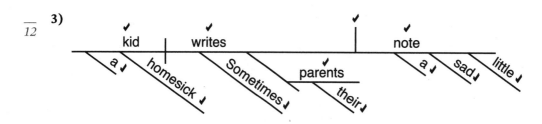

4) $\overline{}$ 6
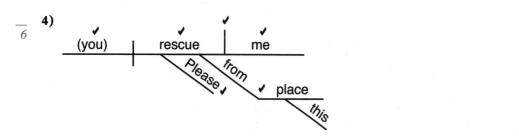

5) $\overline{}$ 8
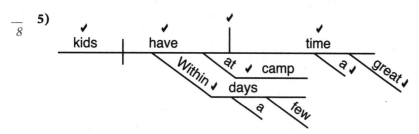

Diagrams

Enter score from diagramming solutions here.

═══ *Total Points*
     38

Lesson 9: Linking Verbs and Sentence Patterns 4 and 5

Exercise A

1)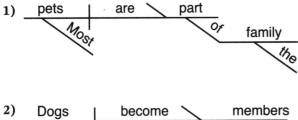

2)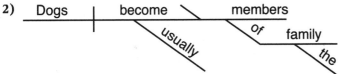

3)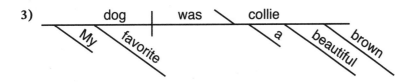

4)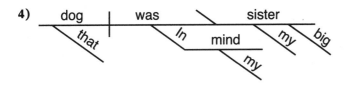

5)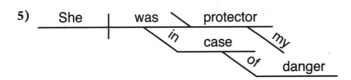

Note: The prepositional phrases *in case* and *of danger* could also modify *protector*. If your student diagrams the sentence this way, do not count it incorrect.

Exercise B

1)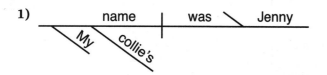

2)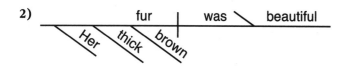

3)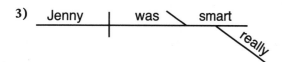

4)

5)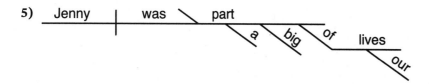

Exercise C

1)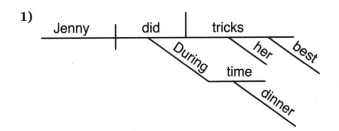

2)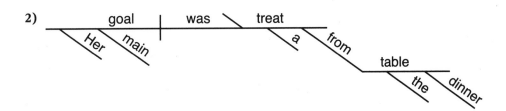

3)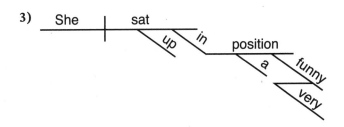

4)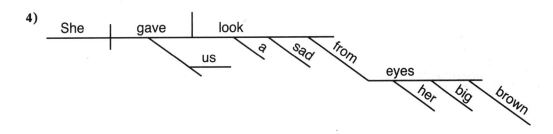

The prepositional phrase from her big brown eyes *could also modify the verb* gave. *If your student diagrams it that way, do not count it incorrect.*

5)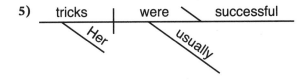

9 DIAGRAMS: ASSESSMENT

Assessment

$\overline{}$ / 7 1)

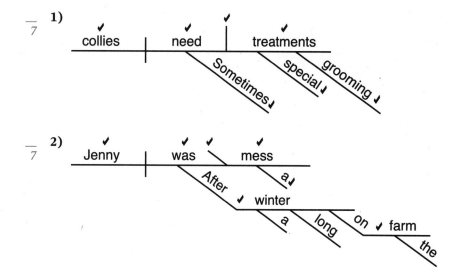

$\overline{}$ / 7 2)

Just as with direct objects, give one point for the slanted line before the predicate nominative or predicate adjective.

$\overline{}$ / 10 3)

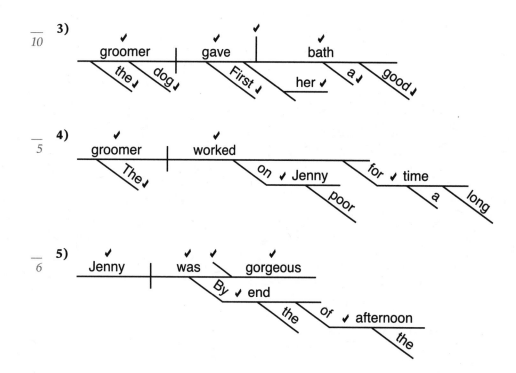

$\overline{}$ / 5 4)

$\overline{}$ / 6 5)

Diagrams

Enter score from diagramming solutions here.

$=$ *Total Points*
35

Lesson 10: Helping Verbs

Exercise A

1)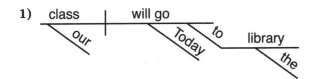

2)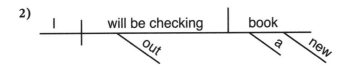

3)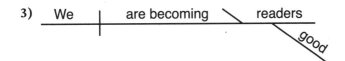

4)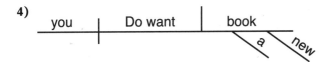

5)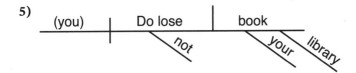

Exercise B

1)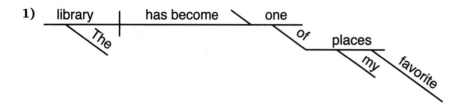

2)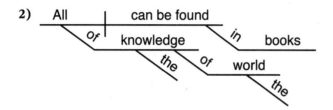

3)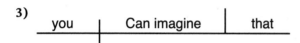

4)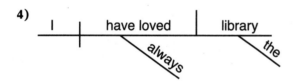

5)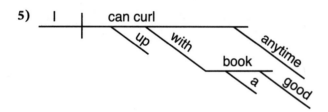

Exercise C

1)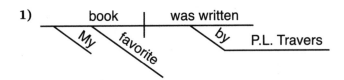

2)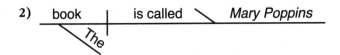

3)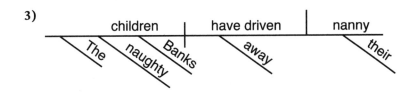

4)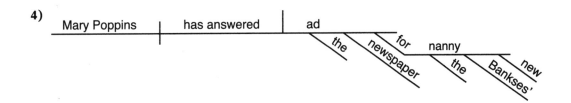

5)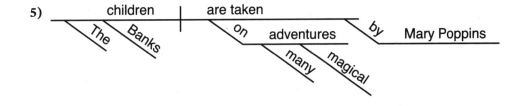

10 Diagrams: Assessment

Assessment

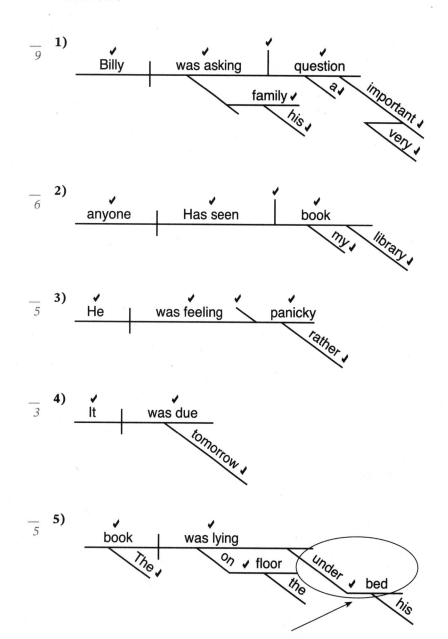

Note: *This prepositional phrase could modify either* was lying *or* floor. *Give credit either way.*

Diagrams

Enter score from diagramming solutions here.

== *Total Points*
28

Lesson 11: Conjunctions and Compounds

Exercise A

1)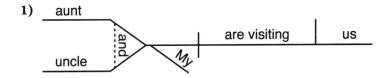

2)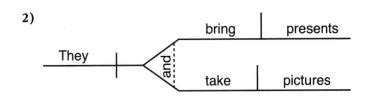

3)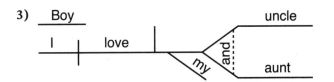

4)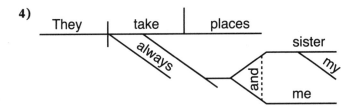

5)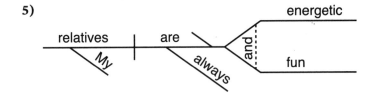

Exercise B

1)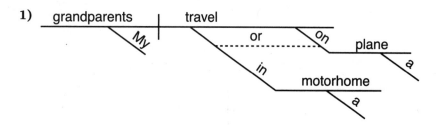

2)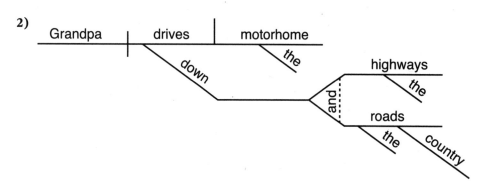

3)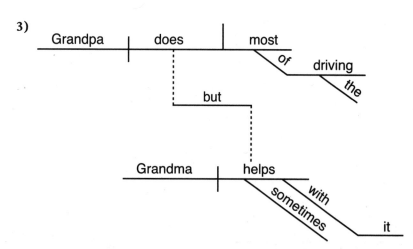

4)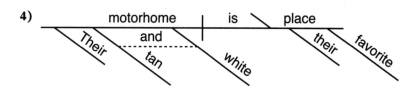

5)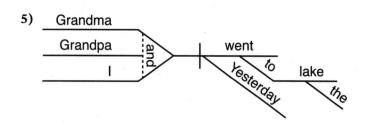

Exercise C

1)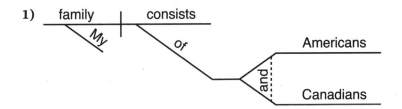

2)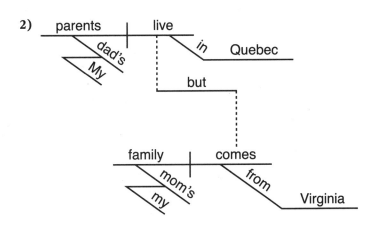

3)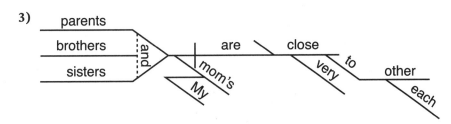

4)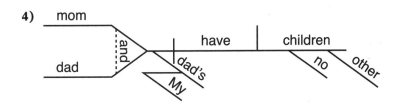

5)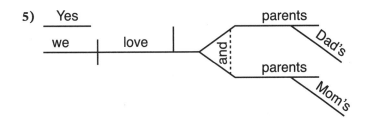

11 DIAGRAMS: ASSESSMENT

Assessment

1)

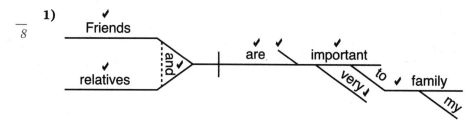

2)

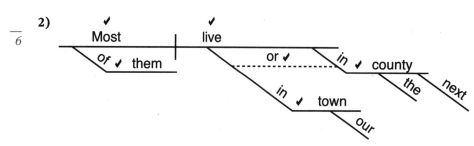

3)

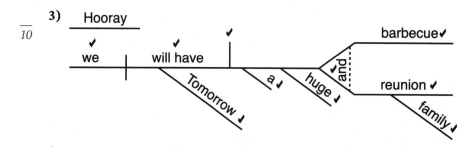

- If your students attach a and huge to barbecue rather than attaching them to the baseline as shown, go ahead and give them credit.

- Award one point of extra credit for correctly diagramming "Hooray!"

4)

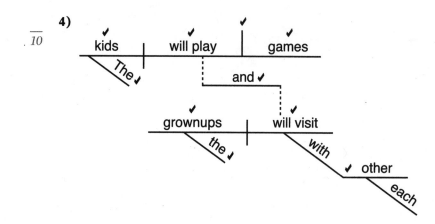

5)

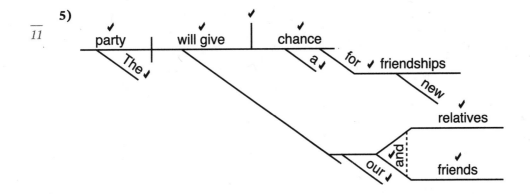

Diagrams

Enter score from diagramming solutions here.

=== Total Points
45

Bibliography

Florey, Kitty Burns. Sister Bernadette's Barking Dog: The Quirky History and Lost Art of Diagramming Sentences. Orlando, FL: Harcourt, 2007.

Garner, Bryan A. Garner's Modern English Usage. Oxford: Oxford University Press, 2016.

Garner, Bryan A. The Chicago Guide to Grammar, Usage, and Punctuation. Chicago, IL: The University of Chicago Press, 2016.

Truss, Lynne. Eats, Shoots & Leaves: The Zero Tolerance Approach to Punctuation. London: Fourth Estate, 2009.